TXTING
2
Talking

Disconnect to Reconnect

KATHRYN HOTTE

Txting 2 Talking
Copyright © 2024 by Kathryn Hotte

Tellwell Talent
www.tellwell.ca

ISBN
978-0-2288-4983-4 (Paperback)
978-1-7794-1971-2 (eBook)

To my mother Valerie who not only supported me through the trials and tribulations of writing this book but life itself.

TABLE OF CONTENTS

ACKNOWLEDGMENTS

This book would not have been possible without the many interviewees who took the time to share their real-life stories and thought-provoking observations. Thank you to the many parents with whom I had energizing and motivating conversations with; I understand your struggle. My appreciation to all the students who attended my Txting 2 Talking workshops and embraced the tech-free philosophy by signing the "No Cell Sunday" pledge, even if they were skeptical at first. A big thank you to my daughter Jenna for supporting me by creating the art piece and taking the photo's that are in this book. Cheers to my family who sometimes still struggle with tech addiction yet are willing to listen and try out some techniques because they understand what I'm talking about!

FOREWORD

"Does this mean that we won't talk to each other anymore?"

My eighty-year-old mother seemed on the verge of tears as my sister and I taught her how to send and receive texts on her smartphone.

"Not at all, Mom," I assured her. "We can still talk on the phone all the time—don't worry about that. Texting is just quicker than calling for small things."

But I empathize with her concern. Would connecting with her children be reduced to quick text notes rather than meaningful conversations? Will I be too quick to text her to say hi rather than taking time to call and chat for a while? It gave me pause to think.

Today, it's a rare person indeed who doesn't text at least some of the time. From young children to senior citizens, almost everyone has the ability and technology to text. And my mom has become great at it—we can text her to let her know we will be ten minutes late, or she can text us when we're at the store to ask us to pick up some whipping cream. We've also been careful to keep talking on the phone and in person. In fact, I've tried to call her even more often now in addition to the occasional quick texts that cover off the small details. But we have to be intentional about it.

This book explores the wonders of modern digital communication— both its practical wonders and its potential pitfalls. And it comes at a crucial time when all of us need reminders of how and why communication is so important.

Good communication is the key to addressing these problems. The challenge is that many people mistake angry rants on social media as effective communication. In fact, it's nearly impossible to engage in intelligent, respectful and informed conversation in 140 characters. As a result, rather than being good communicators, we've allowed ourselves to enter venomous echo chambers. The results have been disastrous.

The world can be a frightening, angry place in the twenty-first century. I suppose the world has always seemed frightening and angry, at least since humans have roamed the earth. Were people any less frightened during the Black Plague in the fourteenth century? Or during the First or Second World Wars? Were people just as anxious during the Cuban Missile Crisis or the financial meltdown of 2008?

Comparisons to other angry, frightening times give us some perspective: we are not the only ones who have worried about an uncertain future. But I'm sure most of us can agree that the world of the 2020s has left many of us emotionally rattled. From the pandemic to politics, and from social division and alternate "truths," it feels like we're on shaky ground.

As an economist, I'm particularly keen to explore the topic of effective communication because our economy relies on it. Farmers must communicate with the buyers of their wheat. Shop owners must communicate the prices and the quality of their products to their customers. Governments and central banks must communicate their intentions to sell or buy government bonds to financial market players. Without solid communication, the economy breaks down quickly.

The most successful players in the economy know how to communicate well. It's called marketing, and it's developed into a science over the last few decades. Sellers can identify their target audience, let them know what they're selling and give their customers the information they need. They can use words ("Extra, extra! Read all about it!"), images (think of the fashion industry), music (remember the Great Root Bear playing his jingle on the tuba?) and even smell (the same distinct white tea scent is present in the lobby of every Westin Hotel in the world).

And in the twenty-first century, marketers also use the ubiquitous texting technology to communicate with customers. By tracking customers' smartphones, some companies now have the creepy ability to locate where their customers are, what they're looking at in the stores and what they've purchased in the past. You may not even know it's happening. But as you walk into the mall, you might get a text from your favourite cosmetics retailer to remind you that you're probably running low on moisturizer.

Is it technology run amuck? Maybe. But rather than smashing your smartphone and swearing off all digital communication, the trick is to harness the best and limit the worst of the technology.

In some ways, the whole of human progress has evolved along a similar storyline. The world of smartphones, texting and digital communication isn't that dissimilar to the first printing press. When books became widely available, they opened up an entirely new world of exciting possibilities for the average person. Writers could communicate to an endless audience, and readers could be transported to different worlds and exposed to new ideas. But a dark side inevitably reared its head: Books could just as easily communicate hatred, lies and depravity. Not everything communicated in a book is positive.

The same split personality exists for more recent technology, including the radio, telephone and television. As a young teen, I sat on the couch watching far too many hours of TV in the 1970s and 1980s. From *M*A*S*H* to *The Muppet Show*, and *Good Times* to *The Golden Girls*, there was a lot to watch. Adults, horrified by the amount of TV my generation watched, shrieked, "They'll never be able to hold a conversation! Their minds will surely turn to mush!"

Yet, our minds didn't turn to mush (or if they did, it probably wasn't due to reruns of *Gilligan's Island*). We did watch too much of "the idiot box," of course, but despite the countless hours in front of the tube, the vast majority of us *did* learn to communicate, to write, to laugh, to love and to be great people. Humans are more resilient and adaptable than we give ourselves credit for.

Still, there is something about technology today that seems more sinister than the pitfalls of the books, radio and television. At least with those other activities, people could engage in the technology together. Some of my best memories of growing up were times spent with my family around the TV, laughing together at *The Carol Burnett Show*.

Texting today is more isolating. True, you text another person, but you're not texting *together*—not in the same way that you'd listen to a radio show or watch a movie together. You're physically separated from the other person, which immediately introduces isolation. Yet for all the potential drawbacks and isolating characteristics of texting and other digital technology, it's here to stay.

That's why this book is so important. We can't be like the Luddites of the 1800s, smashing the machinery of the day because of the threat it posed. We need to embrace texting—but carefully, gingerly. For all its conveniences and advantages, digital communication can be toxic. Above all, we cannot let it replace our human instinct for genuine connection.

I was honoured to write the foreword for this book. It was an enjoyable, thought provoking and insightful read. Kathryn has done her due diligence with her research and the information and statistics shared here. She practices what she preaches.

Todd Hirsch

Todd Hirsch is the former vice president and chief economist for ATB Financial. For more than twenty-five years he has worked as an economist for organizations including the Canada West Foundation and the Bank of Canada.

He is the author of four books. His latest, Spiders in COVID Space: Adapting during and after the pandemic, *was released in March 2021. He serves on the boards of Calgary's Glenbow Museum and the Alberta Ballet. He is also the host of a podcast titled* The Future Of, *which won a national award in 2021.*

INTRODUCTION

Can you read this:

> *MOS I'll BRB. Now DOS OMG SUX! G2G will TXT*
> *L8R TMB. TTFN.*

The answer is most likely yes, at least most of it. If you can't read it, go to Your Dictionary for the translation.[1]

Do you communicate this way via text messages? If so, then congratulations! You are part of the new generation. Even though the English language has evolved over the last few centuries, we are basically going back in time to around 3500 BC when Egyptian hieroglyphics were first used.

Is this something to be celebrated? Didn't evolution expand our vocabulary for a reason? It has been estimated that the English vocabulary includes roughly one million words, and new words are being added all the time.[2] Do we need to decipher another language? Probably not. Are we just lazy? Did we not do well in English class or are we just too busy to write a complete word? Oh, and to make it easier to get the point across, we throw pictures or

---

[1]   Your Dictionary https://grammar.yourdictionary.com/slang/
texting-slang.html Merriam-Websters Dictionary https://www.
merriam-webster.com/help/faq-how-many-english-words. "Your
Dictionary," n.d.

[2]   https://www.merriam-webster.com/help/faq-how-many-english-
words. "Merriam-Websters Dictionary," n.d.

emojis in there as if we are trying to show real emotion since we aren't actually communicating face to face.

I'll admit that I am not a big fan of the new language. Although I resisted for several years, I have realized that texting has become a dominant form of communication, so I've had to adjust. I even drop a smiley face at the end of a text message once in a while! With all the ways to communicate today—and I have adopted most of them—I had hoped to accomplish more by using them, but the opposite has happened.

Why?

I have three e-mail accounts that I have to check daily (yes, I keep them separated) and three voicemails to check (home, business and cell phone). I have several social media sites to update, three websites to maintain, and I text message and use Facebook messenger. I prefer to meet face to face with clients, friends and family because I get so much more clarity, interaction and things accomplished when I can speak directly with them rather than via text or e-mail. That being said, I have been told that I communicate well and that I have a flair for the art of communication when many others have difficulty. I have personally seen and interviewed many young individuals who have difficulty communicating face to face. Many are socially inept and have increased social anxiety when in large groups.

And this is getting worse.

When I started writing this book, I thought I would complete it in a year. That was eight years ago. I refused to get my thirteen-year-old son a phone at the time, and he has now graduated from college. Of course, I did eventually buy him a cell phone, but I was worried that he might become like many of his friends, ignore me when I speak to him, text at the table during Christmas dinner or learn a new tech language when he hadn't even mastered the one he was currently using. Frankly, I was already competing with video games, so I didn't need another distraction. Although some of those things do happen today, he has learned to communicate well and is socially active. In fact, he attended a couple of my networking events and made quite a few connections and contacts.

When he was around 10 I asked him to accompany me to one of my monthly networking events of which I was the president. It was a Christmas party, and we had a medieval troupe entertain us so he was happy to help out by greeting the guests as they arrived as well as taking their plates when they were finished eating. He wore his suit so he could look the part of a young professional, and I versed him on how to shake hands and greet the guests. I had a young woman from the troupe approach me towards the end of the evening and say, "Your son is the most sweet and polite boy I have ever been around. He was so helpful and really has a way of talking with people. You must be very proud." I was proud, and I received this type of feedback regularly. Years later, teachers, friends, family and business associates still share their fondness for this kid.

In this book I will shed some light on the texting and messaging epidemic that is sweeping the world and affecting how we, and especially our youth, communicate. I aim to bring awareness to what is actually happening to our communication skills and how digital technology is affecting us. I hope to inspire you to get back to the basics by learning how to effectively communicate face to face.

Texting, e-mail, social media messaging, webcasts, video, voicemail are all useful, and I'm not advocating ignoring technology. However, humans must interact on a physical level using the five senses because our bodies are built this way. Hearing a human voice rather than reading a text creates a stronger bond between people. Giving a hug and soft words of encouragement to a crying friend rather than sending a dehumanizing emoji means you are really present and there for support. In a world where texting is replacing phone calls or face-to-face meetings, should we worry that evolution may eliminate our voice boxes? The act of speaking should be our cherished possession, and if we stop using it at some point, it could be taken away.

I have exhaustively researched where we started, how we got here, problems we are facing and where can we go from here. I'm self-taught and have a British background, so I am steeped in politeness and good manners. Maybe it was all that tea that my mother nourished us with. With my extensive and varied background in managing teams as well as training and facilitating various workshops on many topics including communication, I have been around the block a few times and learned what to do and what not to do.

I have structured *Txting 2 Talking* to emphasize a diversity of viewpoints. I reached out to individuals from around the world with various backgrounds and perspectives to find out what they think. As well, I wanted to give you the opportunity to think about the themes and topics, apply real thought to your life circumstances and maybe even take some action. You will see the following icons throughout the book:

 Interviews: What do you say?

 To sum it up, ponder and now over to you

 Put a pin in it! Practice tips you can do right away!

 Hmmm… Makes you think!

My goal is for you to enjoy *Txting 2 Talking* so much so that you call up a friend or relative and take them for a coffee and a chat—face to face!

Kathryn Hotte
Spring 2023

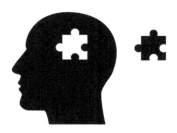

CHAPTER ONE
———

Is There a Problem?

The single biggest problem in communication is the illusion that it has taken place.

George Bernard Shaw

I started writing this book in 2013, and every time I returned to it, I had to research again and again because the tech world changes at the speed of light. When I did an Internet search for "Internet & texting addictions" back in 2013 I received 1.8 million results. I searched the same information in 2018 and received over fourteen million results. I did this again in 2021 and got over sixteen million results. A huge difference in eight years.

Do we really have a problem? Are we addicted to our phones, the Internet and social media?

We are used having our devices with us 24/7 with access to anything anytime from anywhere. We have become complacent and accustomed to it. Maybe we are guilty of looking at our phone every five minutes or scrolling through social media one more time—or for the tenth time today—to see what everyone is up to. Do we tell our kids to get off the computer or put their phone down when we are in the middle of a Facebook post? It's like when an adult would say, "Don't smoke, it's bad for you," as they butt out their cigarette. Some of us listened, some of us didn't.

In this chapter, we are going to explore whether we have a problem by completing some quick self-assessments. There are a ton out there that you can complete online whether you are a parent or a teen, and the addictions are everything from what we are showing here to other areas like video games, gambling and even sexting and pornography.

So, let's start with our phones. Are we addicted? Are our kids addicted?

Are you "Nomophobic"? NO MObile PHOne phoBIA is a twenty-first-century term for the fear of not being able to access your cell phone or other smart device. Take the test and then ask another member of the family to try.[3]

Rate your responses on a scale of 1 (strongly disagree) to 7 (strongly agree) and add your score.

Indicate how much you agree or disagree with each statement in relation to your smartphone						
Strongly Disagree			Neutral			Strongly Agree
1	2	3	4	5	6	7
1. I would feel uncomfortable without constant access to information through my smartphone						
2. I would be annoyed if I could not look up information on my smartphone when I wanted to						
3. Being unable to get the news (e.g., happenings, weather, etc.) on my smartphone would make me nervous						
4. I would be annoyed if I could not use my smartphone and/ or its capabilities when I wanted to						
5. My smartphone running out of battery would scare me						
6. If I were to run out of credits or hit my monthly data limit, I would panic						
7. If I did not have a data signal or could not connect to Wi-Fi, I would constantly check to see if I had a signal or could find a Wi-Fi network						
8. If I could not use my smartphone, I would be afraid of getting stranded somewhere						
9. If I could not check my smartphone for a while, I would feel a desire to check it						
10. If I did not have my smartphone with me, I would feel anxious because I could not instantly communicate with my family and/or friends						

---

[3] Yildirim, C. & Correia, A. (2015). Exploring the dimensions of nomophobia: Development and validation of a self-reported questionnaire. *Computers in Human Behavior, 49*, 130-137

11. If I did not have my smartphone with me, I would be worried because my family and/or friends could not reach me	
12. If I did not have my smartphone with me, I would feel nervous because I would not be able to receive text messages and calls	
13. If I did not have my smartphone with me, I would be anxious because I could not keep in touch with my family and/or friends	
14. If I did not have my smartphone with me, I would be nervous because I could not know if someone had tried to get a hold of me	
15. If I did not have my smartphone with me, I would feel anxious because my constant connection to my family and friends would be broken	
16. If I did not have my smartphone with me, I would be nervous because I would be disconnected from my online identity	
17. If I did not have my smartphone with me, I would be uncomfortable because I could not stay up to date with social media and online networks	
18. If I did not have my smartphone with me, I would feel awkward because I could not check my notifications for updates from my connections and online networks	
19. If I did not have my smartphone with me, I would feel anxious because I could not check my e-mail messages	
20. If I did not have my smartphone with me, I would feel weird because I would not know what to do	
Total	

What was your score?

20 or lower: No nomophobia

21–59: Mild nomophobia

60–99: Moderate nomophobia

100–140: Severe nomophobia

According to Caglar Yildirim, the assistant professor of human computer interaction who created the scale for use in his research at State University of New York at Oswego, score of twenty or below means you're not an addict; a score of twenty-one to sixty means you're mildly nomophobic, and a score of sixty-one to ninety-nine means you probably can't go long without checking your phone.

"It might be a good idea to be conscious of that," Yildirim said, "but we are only concerned if it starts to interfere with your daily life."

If you scored over one hundred, you're probably struggling with severe anxiety when you can't access your cell phone. "This might negatively affect your social life and relationships with friends and family," Yildirim said. "There are studies that show those who score high on the test tend to avoid face-to-face interactions, have high levels of social anxiety and maybe even depression."

Kim Silverthorn, Therapist. BA, RPC, MPCC, CT
Owner/Operator of Tacit Knowledge Counselling and
Mental Health Training
Canada

For me, technology changes over the past ten years or so have been a double-edged sword. Because the world has been changing as a whole, the option to not adapt is not a productive one. But not being raised with these technological aspects as a way of life has been a bit of a struggle for my brain, and while I want to keep up, it doesn't always come naturally/easily to me. Having the ease of instant communication—from texts to videos to FaceTime to e-mails and photos—with the people I care about is wonderful. It's fun, it's a great connection tool and it allows me to connect more frequently and maintain more of a relationship with the people in my circle than ever before. Having technology at my fingertips when I travel, while I wait between meetings or appointments and when I need information quickly is a godsend both as a distraction and an aid, and it has saved my butt on many occasions. Time is maximized in so many ways.

However, there has been a learning curve as I have come to realize that the trust I put in the technology that is so readily available is often misplaced. False information, misconstrued facts and inaccurate/outdated information is far too prevalent. And sometimes being able to tell what is fact and what is not can be next to impossible, which leads me to doubt (perhaps wisely) even more in what I read/see/hear about in all of the messages/information I gather. The new language of communication through technology has been a road fraught with misunderstanding, and learning to interpret the messages is a whole new skill set I was not born into so I have to learn through trial and error. Some of my trust has been damaged instead of strengthened along the way.

Because I've had a foot in both worlds, I still also enjoy my Luddite moments. I read print publications, enjoy long telephone conversations and in-person visits more than technologically driven connections, and I handwrite letters and send cards by Canada Post. I seem to forget my phone at home just as often as I remember to take it with me, and I unplug from technology completely for at least ten to twelve hours a day with no adverse side effects except peace of mind and a sense of full relaxation. These practices still bring me joy, they offer a glimpse of my personality in a more intimate manner and help define who I am in ways that I don't think technology ever could.

But I enjoy the convenience and the immediacy of the new technological world just as much but in different ways. I am grateful to be so actively connected to my son, who attends university three provinces away, through the running dialogue we have throughout the day. I am grateful for the immediacy of the help I need when I am in unsafe or stressful situations. And I am grateful for the connection I have to a world that might be quite isolating for me without the technological advances over the past ten years.

As far as impacts I've seen in my practice, most of my clients are comfortable with technology and will often attend sessions with their devices perched on the couch beside them. For some, this connection to their lives during their personal therapeutic time is a safety practice and allows them peace of mind (and the ability to focus on themselves more completely) by knowing the sitter/kids are not in crisis. Others' devices bring a distraction that limits their ability to focus on their emotional needs to the degree that the therapy offers and is perhaps a safety practice protecting them against their own vulnerability when they are not quite ready to delve into that state.

Beyond their presence in session, almost all of my clients have grown far more dependent upon their devices as the years progress. In many ways, the use of technology as a positive tool/aid in their lives is beneficial. It allows them to be more organized, to save time and to clarify things much faster. Specifically related to their counselling process, clients use technology to confirm and set appointments, pay for their sessions, as a notepad for details they want to share in therapy, and to create reminders of homework and resources they can access outside of the counselling office. But at times, the technology becomes a crutch (creating a dependency on an external mechanism rather than an internal reliance on self), an addiction (an unhealthy coping strategy for challenging times/feelings) and/or an extension of their identity in a way that is controlling and damaging (their value/worth is viewed through aspects of technology that are not true indicators of who they are/want to be as a person). There is a struggle to disconnect and balance responsibility and pressures (work, family, social connections) and to allow alone time/downtime—an almost constant fear of "missing out" or falling behind. There is an absence of boredom/still time which leaves less room for the healthy development of imagination and self-reflection.

With youth especially, the idea of being without constant access to their device is almost a foreign concept—one that usually elicits panic and anger and confusion. Tech access has become an extension of their own human self—a new appendage of sorts—a need (not just a desire) that, if unmet, causes emotional, mental and physical deterioration (to varying degrees, depending upon a few different factors). There is also often a false belief that one "knows" real life experiences simply because one has come across something similar through a device (video games, online or via social media—especially someone else's). And this false sense of self-awareness tends to stagnate true personal growth by limiting a youth's desire/recognition of the need to live experiences first-hand.

In my experience, as the use of devices grows and the in-person, face-to-face interactions between people shrinks, so does our ability to successfully communicate and to fully appreciate one another. Our sense of humanity is diminished. Our ability to both demonstrate and to accept interpersonal connection on a deeper level is compromised. Emotional resonance cannot be experienced without in-person interactions, and our natural ability to understand and trust our own selves in relation to others (through an awareness of our "gut instinct," for example) is also minimized to a large degree. As we lose our empathy and our compassion for and with one another (because technology provides a false front behind which many of us hide, for varying reasons), we lose more connection to/awareness of ourselves. Although technology seems to offer an increased opportunity for these connections, the loss of the humanity within the process has resulted in the opposite effect.

When you hear the words of a practiced and respected therapist talk about our "need" (especially our youth's need) to be connected to our devices at all times, and that without our devices we panic or get angry we need to listen. The fact that almost all of our communication is conducted without any face-to-face interactions warrants a look at our loss of empathy, consideration, understanding and tolerance. It is easier to hide behind a text message because there is no need for emotion unless you consider an emoji a relevant reaction.

Internet Addiction

We cannot look at smartphone addiction and not also look at Internet addiction since we can access anything from our phone. The Internet is a fabulous tool we use all the time. I can search for anything at any time anywhere, so where does the addiction kick in? Let's look at the quick assessment below.

Signs of Internet Addiction

1. Do you feel preoccupied with the Internet (think about previous online activity or anticipate your next online session)?
2. Do you feel the need to use the Internet for increasing amounts of time in order to achieve satisfaction?
3. Have you repeatedly made unsuccessful efforts to control, cut back or stop Internet use?
4. Do you feel restless, moody, depressed or irritable when attempting to cut down or stop Internet use?
5. Do you stay online longer than you intended?
6. Have you jeopardized or risked the loss of a significant relationship, job, educational or career opportunity because of the Internet?
7. Have you lied to family members, a therapist or others to conceal the extent of involvement with the Internet?
8. Do you use the Internet as a way of escaping from problems or of relieving a dysphoric mood (e.g., feelings of helplessness, guilt, anxiety, depression)?

If you selected five of the eight criteria from the Internet Addiction Diagnostic Questionnaire (IADQ),[4] it means you are addicted.

Social Media

Many of us are guilty of checking our social media sites because it's our way of connecting and reconnecting. The most popular by far is Facebook with almost three billion monthly users.

I've made a concerted effort to cut down my constant "check in" rate on my Facebook page and unfortunately have missed a few

---

[4]   eMental Health.ca https://www.ementalhealth.ca/index. php?m=survey&ID=47. "eMental Health.Ca," n.d.

birthdays and events that are outside of my immediate circle. However, I was surprised when a colleague asked why I didn't attend an event.

"I didn't know about it," I said.

"Well, it was posted on Facebook," she said.

Well not everyone is constantly on Facebook, I thought.

This is a great Facebook addiction test I found via Tech Addiction.[5]

Facebook Addiction Test	True	False
1. I often spend too much time on Facebook—usually more than I originally intend.		
2. I am often tired in the morning because I stay up late on Facebook.		
3. My friends or family have commented that I spend too much time on Facebook.		
4. I spend more than two hours per day on Facebook for non-work-related reasons.		
5. I often use Facebook at work or school even though this is not permitted.		
6. I would find it very difficult if I could not access my Facebook account for an entire day.		
7. I have made an effort to collect as many "friends" as possible on Facebook.		
8. Many of my Facebook friends are not really my friends offline.		
9. My work or school performance has suffered due to too much Facebook use.		
10. My relationships have suffered due to too much Facebook use.		
11. I often spend hours at a time playing games on Facebook.		

---

[5]   facebook-addiction-test-symptoms.html. "Facebook Addiction Test," n.d.

12. When I post an update on Facebook, I am very disappointed if no one comments on it.		
13. I usually prefer talking to people on Facebook than in person.		
14. I have attempted to reduce the amount of time I spend on Facebook but have not been successful.		
15. I spend more time using Facebook compared to any other online activity.		
16. I often use Facebook to avoid other responsibilities (e.g., work, homework, housework, etc.).		
17. Since starting to use Facebook I spend less time doing other activities I used to enjoy (e.g., sports, exercise, socializing with others, hobbies, etc.).		
18. Even though I have many Facebook friends, I still feel lonely.		
19. I often login to Facebook when I am out socially with others.		
20. Checking my Facebook account is one of the first things I do in the morning.		
21. Checking my Facebook account is one of the last things I do at night.		
22. I use Facebook when I am feeling stressed or depressed to make me feel better.		
23. I am often late for school, work, meetings or appointments because of my Facebook use.		
24. I would get very upset if a friend did not "add" me to Facebook.		
25. I have set my Facebook account so that I get always automatic notifications about what my friends are doing/saying.		
26. It makes me feel bad if I know that someone has more Facebook friends than I do.		
27. I think it would be virtually impossible for me to give up Facebook for an entire month.		
28. I often confuse what someone has told me in "real life" and what was said on Facebook.		
29. I often use Facebook when I am bored because I have nothing else to do.		

Scoring: Total your "TRUES" and see below for score interpretation.

Interpretation:

Of the twenty-nine questions above, how many did you answer as "True"?

While there is no set number that indicates an addiction to Facebook, the more often you agreed with the above signs of overuse, the more likely it is that your Facebook habits are excessive or unhealthy.

0–5: You are most likely a light user of Facebook. You can take it or leave it, and it probably does not cause any significant problems in your life.

6–10: Facebook is a part of your daily routine. At times you may spend too much time with it and may regret long Facebook sessions after you finally log off.

11–20: Your use of Facebook may be unhealthy or obsessive. Too much time on Facebook may be causing or contributing to "real life" problems, and you may use it to avoid other important responsibilities.

21+: Your life revolves around Facebook. You would find it very difficult to go more than a day or two without checking your account. Your relationships and your school or work performance are probably suffering due to excessive Facebook use.

Kelly Ann Reiss
Editor, Journalist, Documentary Film-maker
Canada
A Media/Film Perspective

As a journalist and editor, I have found that today's technology has added to my workload. I must respond to people's e-mails before I can have a conversation with them. Around fifteen years ago when I started in the business there was no Facebook or smartphones. When I was out, I was out, and people didn't get upset when they couldn't get a hold of me right away. People today feel they can reach me anytime. I get texts at 6:30 in the morning asking me if I can attend an event that day, and if I don't get back right away they feel "put off." I get into the back and forth with e-mails, and its so much easier to just call and speak over the phone it certainly takes less time.

Before phones, I had to problem solve and make up my own systems, today we are always looking for information on our phones because there may be a better way to do something. Previously, I had to go to the library and read a book. Today I can research forever; there's no bottom, no end, and everything's available all the time. I'm sure sometimes we procrastinate because we know it will be a while to complete something because we can read and read, it doesn't end..

My parents are in their seventies and like to Facebook message me and my brother, however, I'd prefer it if they'd just call and have a conversation with me. My mother is a Twitter troll and seems to get into arguments with people about politics. On a recent trip to Australia, she had to take two hours to catch up with her Twitter community once we arrived there.

My sister has two small kids aged nine months and two years, and I see how quickly they adapt to technology. They have very little screen time, but when they go into a room where there's a screen, they are naturally drawn to it. The older one is into books because my sister made a point of reading to him, but if he sees someone with a phone he'll run to them and try to take it out of their hand. If he gets to watch something and you turn it off, he cries. Before he was a year old he knew how to skip the ads on YouTube—the technology is so intuitive that a baby can figure it out.

We never had Facebook when we were kids, so how do you parent that? Kids make mistakes they don't have any strong sense of right or wrong or of the consequences. For example, you hear of the bullying or posting photos that they probably shouldn't and when it's online it is amplified, We all do something stupid when we're young but now it's accessible, it's out there. When I covered politics, the opposition would go through Twitter feeds years back, find something questionable on a candidate and send it to local media. You have to be really careful and realize that if people want to get you, they will find something.

As far as the younger generation is concerned, I find teens are too cool for anything, and they try to avoid making eye contact. I worked with a young man and didn't get a chance to really get to know him. We had to take a car trip and I thought this was a good time to connect, but he was on his phone for the whole trip. I'll go for a professional lunch with a younger person, which is a chance for them to network, and they'll be on their phone the entire time so they don't know how to network. At a casual dinner you can't have a basic conversation because as soon as someone says something like, "What's that actor's name again?" it turns to, "Oh, let's look it up." Then everyone whips out their phones and starts scrolling. They don't have to think or remember anything. Look at phones, for example. The younger generation doesn't know personal phone numbers, (I'll admit I'm guilty too). If I ever forgot my phone at home and needed to contact my husband I wouldn't know his number. We don't have landline phones anymore, so even in an emergency 911 situation police can't pinpoint you exactly unless you have a landline. Minutes can cost a life. Many emergency workers have landlines.

Will people care about having their information out there in the future? It may go the other way. Maybe people will start to opt out of Facebook and other social media sites, and I've heard some say that they are happier that they quit Facebook because they actually read a book because they are not scrolling for an hour. I've gone on to the Internet to look up something then forgot what I was looking for because I clicked on a video and got distracted. But if you quit Facebook or other social media, you do you lose being connected to everyone.

Being and editor and journalist, Kelly Ann has conducted her share of interviews over the years, so her experience has given her a unique perspective that I resonate with since I started my research. It is interesting that I found more people who are opting out of social media than ever before. Will they find something to replace it? My hope is that whatever they replace their time with, it is not spent on another device.

Americans Are Changing Their Relationship with Facebook
By Andrew Perrin, Pew Research Center
September 5, 2018

Significant shares of Facebook users have taken steps in the past year to reframe their relationship with the social media platform. Just over half of Facebook users ages 18 and older (54%) say they have adjusted their privacy settings in the past 12 months, according to a new Pew Research Center survey. Around four in ten (42%) say they have taken a break from checking the platform for a period of several weeks or more, while around a quarter (26%) say they have deleted the Facebook app from their cell phone. All told, some 74% of Facebook users say they have taken at least one of these three actions in the past year.

The findings come from a survey of U.S. adults conducted May 29-June 11, following revelations that the former consulting firm Cambridge Analytica had collected data on tens of millions of Facebook users without their knowledge.

 So how did you do?

You can't move forward until you know where you are today.

Did your scores surprise you?

I encourage you to share the self-assessments with your family and friends and then discuss the impact it may be having on your lives.

The two things that I noticed, and the reason why I embarked on this journey, were:

1. With all the technology we have at our fingertips, very little of it involves us actually speaking; and
2. We are the most globally connected human race in history, but we are becoming the most disconnected in human-to-human, face-to-face contact.

In the next chapter, we will explore the origins of how the disconnection all started. It's easy to see the evolution of things when the historical timeline is laid out for you because it gives you a different perspective and, I hope, a new understanding of how we got here.

CHAPTER TWO

How Did It All Start?
A Brief History of
Communication as
We Know It

The great challenge facing us today is to learn once again how to talk to one another, not simply how to generate and consume information. The latter is a tendency which our important and influential modern communications media can encourage. Information is important, but it is not enough. All too often things get simplified, different positions and viewpoints are pitted against one another, and people are invited to take sides rather than to see things as a whole.

Pope Francis

The main difference between animals and us is the fact that we can speak and they can't. Sure, a dog can bark and nod towards the cupboard that has the bones in it, but he can't sing the national anthem. Apparently, it's physically impossible for animals to speak; birds are an exception, but they produce sound differently. In his book titled Eve Spoke, evolutionist Philip Lieberman stated, "Speech is so essential to our concept of intelligence that its possession is virtually equated with being human. Animals who talk are human, because what sets us apart from other animals is the 'gift' of speech."[6]

We are not only able to speak, but we are also able to speak at an early age and at an amazing rate. Sure, we can't walk as soon as we are born like a horse can, for example, but we can ask for "Da Da" at six months old, respond to our own name and use the tone of our voice to let everyone know that we are happy or sad by the seven month mark. By twelve months we respond to simple requests like "Put that down," and by eighteen months we know simple words, can point to people and objects and repeat words that people say. As information scientist Werner Gitt observed in his book *The Wonder of Man*, "By the age of six, the average child has learned to use and understand about 13,000 words; by eighteen it will have a working vocabulary of 60,000 words. That means it has been learning an average of ten new words a day since its first birthday, the equivalent of a new word every ninety minutes of its waking life."[7]

---

[6]   Eve Spoke: Human Language and Human Evolution, Philip Lieberman 1998

[7]   *The Wonder of Man Werner Gitt 1996*

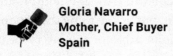 **Gloria Navarro**
Mother, Chief Buyer
Spain

A Parent's Perspective

Technology has influenced my way of living and communicating professionally and personally.

My husband and I control screen time in our family and try to avoid allowing our six-year-old daughter on screens because we think it is critical to develop social interactions until she is fourteen instead of screen interactions. We are also very concerned about her properly developing her handwriting because keyboards may decrease her handwriting capabilities. At home we use only TV and computers to work or for homework (yes, at the age of six the school prescribes homework done on tablets). We decided to retire the tablets (we have three iPads and two e-readers) in favour of TV and shared screens.

What concerns me as a parent is the decrease in reading time and handwriting, the amount of screen time and the isolation it presents, socially and mentally. I notice in my daughter's case a lack of focus on one task.

I think it is still too early to determine the future impact on the next generation, however, lack of critical thinking and lack of focus will probably determine our future behaviour.

Andreas Kanther
University Professor, Father
Elche, Spain

Technology has affected me a lot. Today most of my work would be impossible without being connected to the Internet. E-mail and web searches are essential for my work. Texting and messaging are being used but not so essential. It affects my private life more than my professional life.

In my personal life, instead of calling someone or being called, now WhatsApp is used. Sometimes for better and sometimes for worse. The advantage is that you can attend to the messages when it is convenient for you, whereas a phone call has to be attended to at that moment. The negative part is that there are fewer conversations by phone, which is more personal and "touching" than the messaging.

I use messaging with my wife, and it is very convenient to pass information in a less intrusive way. I do not use it with my daughter since she is only six years old and does not have a smartphone.

People have a great attachment to their devices and the impact is enormous. Younger people especially seem to have a reduced attention span in part because of the mobile devices they are using. For many of them, incoming messages have to be attended to immediately, so they are distracted often and lose the ability to focus on a single task over a longer time period. It has affected face-to-face communication since many conversations are interrupted by an incoming message and people get nervous when they have not looked at their smartphone for a long time.

As far as the future is concerned, I see an impact. We get many tiny bits of information or news, which makes it impossible sometimes to see the overall picture and put things in context. I agree with my wife: The inability to focus on a single task will have consequences especially in a work environment when focus on a specific task is needed to be productive in achieving objectives.

Gloria and Andreas realize that with their own pile of devices it is difficult to escape the attachment to them and everything that comes with that. No matter how it all started, this is the reality of their lives, and a conscious effort needs to be made to detach and disconnect. However, even that comes with consequences, especially in a work environment. As parents, they understand that even at the young age of six their daughter is already experiencing a world without handwriting and she is encouraged to use a tablet for homework. They are worried about a reduced focus on one task which warrants a look at multitasking. Will not knowing how to handwrite a letter really matter? Is the need to focus on only one task realistic now that the pace of information is speeding up? Don't we need to multitask? Throughout history we are known to lose a skill and gain a new one only to find out that the old skill is actually better. Multitasking, for example, is constantly being debated. Is it really productive or is efficiency and performance impacted because your brain can only focus on one thing at a time?

Author and computer science professor Cal Newport wrote the books *Deep Work* and *Digital Minimalism: Choosing a Focused Life in a Digital World* to explore these impacts and their consequences. In *Deep Work*, Cal proposed that in order to do our best work and live a purposeful life, we need to be intentional with how we spend our time. In *Digital Minimalism*, he looks at how we can become a digital minimalist and rebuild our relationship with technology so that it serves us, not the other way around. The search term "Be more productive and focus" generates 183 million search results. There is a strong following and growing business around this topic it ponders us to think, why are we all struggling with the lack of ability to focus?

So here we are with the complete capability to communicate at an early age, and beyond, using something that is already built in and not paid for, our unique voices. We can spend hundreds of dollars on a gym membership or thousands on gym equipment yet most fitness trainers will tell you that you possess everything you need to keep your body in shape. Jumping jacks don't require specialized equipment, and running doesn't require the need of a credit card. Well, OK, maybe the Nike shoes do!

Talk is cheap! It costs you nothing and doesn't require a three-year unlimited texting plan. Plus, communication is more effective one-on-one than via a text or an e-mail (more on that in Chapter Five).

How did we get to a place where we are more than willing to pay to communicate? Where did we come from? How did it all start? Let's look at the major milestones in the history of communication.

Time Period	Communication Milestone
	BC
3500–2900	The Phoenicians develop an alphabet. The Sumerians develop cuneiform writing (pictographs of accounts written on clay tablets). The Egyptians develop hieroglyphic writing.
1775	Greeks use a phonetic alphabet written from left to right.
1400	Oldest record of writing in China on bones.
1270	The first encyclopedia is written in Syria.
900	The first postal service (for government use) in China.
776	First recorded use of homing pigeons used to send message (the winner of the Olympic Games to the Athenians).
530	The Greeks start the first library.
500–170	Papyrus rolls and early parchment made of dried reeds becomes the first portable and light writing surfaces.

200–100	Human messengers on foot or horseback common in Egypt and China with messenger relay stations built. Sometimes fire messages used from relay station to station instead of humans.
	14: Romans establish postal services.
	37: Heliographs are the first recorded use of mirrors to send messages by Roman Emperor Tiberius.
	100: First bound books
105	Tsai Lun of China invents paper as we know it.
AD	
305	First wooden printing presses invented in China (symbols carved on a wooden block).
1049	First movable type (clay) invented in China by Pi Sheng.
1450	Newspapers appear in Europe.
1455	Johannes Gutenberg invents a printing press with metal movable type.
1560	Camera obscura (primitive image making) invented.
1650	First daily newspaper, Leipzig, Germany.
1714	Englishmen Henry Mill receives the first patent for a typewriter.
1793	Claude Chappe invents the first long-distance semaphore (visual or optical) telegraph line.
The 19th Century	
1814	Joseph Nicéphore Niépce achieves the first photographic image.
1821	Charles Wheatstone reproduces sound in a primitive sound box; the first microphone.
1831	Joseph Henry invents the first electric telegraph.
1835	Samuel Morse invents Morse code.

1843	Samuel Morse invents the first long-distance electric telegraph line. Alexander Bain patents the first fax machine.
1861	United States starts the Pony Express for mail delivery. Coleman Sellers invents the Kinematoscope, which was a machine that flashed a series of still photographs onto a screen.
1867	American Christopher Latham Sholes invents the first modern typewriter.
1876	Thomas Edison patents the mimeograph, an office copying machine. Alexander Graham Bell patents the electric telephone. Melvil Dewey creates the Dewey Decimal System for ordering library books.
1877	Thomas Edison patents the phonograph with a wax cylinder as recording medium. Eadweard Muybridge invents high-speed photography, creating first moving pictures that captured motion.
1887	Emile Berliner invents the gramophone, a system of recording which could be used over and over again.
1888	George Eastman patents Kodak roll film camera.
1889	Almon Strowger patents the direct dial telephone (automatic telephone exchange).
1894	Guglielmo Marconi improves wireless telegraphy.
1898	First telephone answering machines.
1899	Valdemar Poulsen invents the first magnetic recordings using magnetized steel tape as recording medium. This is the foundation for mass data storage on disk and tape and the music recording industry. Loudspeakers invented.

The Twentieth Century	
1902	Guglielmo Marconi transmits radio signals from Cornwall to Newfoundland, the first radio signal across the Atlantic Ocean.
1904	First regular comic books.
1906	Lee Deforest invents the electronic amplifying tube or triode. This allowed all electronic signals to be amplified, improving all electronic communications (i.e., telephones and radios).
1910	Thomas Edison demonstrated the first talking motion picture.
1914	First cross continental telephone call made.
1916	First radios with tuners, different stations.
1923	Vladimir Kosma Zworykin invents the television or iconoscope (cathode ray tube); first television camera.
1925	John Logie Baird transmits the first experimental television signal.
1926	Warner Brothers Studios invents a way to record sound separately from the film on large disks and synchronize the sound and motion picture tracks upon playback; an improvement on Thomas Edison's work.
1927	NBC starts two radio networks. CBS is founded. First television broadcasts in England. Warner Brothers releases *The Jazz Singer*, the first feature film and talking motion picture.
1930	Radio popularity spreads with the "Golden Age" of radio. First television broadcasts in the United States. Movietone system of recording film sound on an audio track right on the film invented.
1934	Joseph Begun invents the first tape recorder for broadcasting; first magnetic recording.
1938	Television broadcasts able to be taped and edited rather than only live.

1939	Scheduled television broadcasts begin.
1944	Computers like Harvard's Mark I put into public service (government owned).
	The age of information science begins.
1948	Long playing record invented; vinyl and played at 33⅓ rpm.
	Transistor invented enabling the miniaturization of electronic devices.
1949	Network television starts in the United States.
	45 rpm record invented.
1951	Computers are first sold commercially.
1958	Chester Carlson invents the photocopier or Xerox machine.
	Integrated Circuit invented enabling the further miniaturization of electronic devices and computers.
1963	Zip codes invented in the United States.
1966	Xerox invents the Telecopier, the first successful fax machine.
1969	ARPANET—the first Internet—started.
1971	The computer floppy disc invented.
	The microprocessor invented; considered a computer on a chip.
	E-mail first developed by Ray Tomlinson.
1972	HBO invents pay-TV service for cable.
1973	The first transatlantic connection.
	E-mail accounts for 75 percent of all ARPANET network activity.
1975	The first modern e-mail program enabling reply and forwarding is invented.

1976	Apple I home computer invented. First nationwide (US) programming via satellite invented and implemented by Ted Turner.
1977	The first PC modem developed by Dennis Hayes and Dale Heatherington; initially sold to computer hobbyists.
1978	Spam is born and the first unsolicited commercial e-mail message sent out to six hundred California ARPANET users by Gary Thuerk.
1979	First cellular phone communication network started in Japan. *MultiUser Dungeon* (MUD) becomes the earliest form of multiplayer games. The precursor to *World of Warcraft* and *Second Life*. Text-based virtual worlds, combining elements of role-playing games, interactive, fiction and online chat are invented. Usenet, an Internet-based discussion system allowing people from around the globe to converse about the same topics by posting public messages categorized by newsgroups, is created by two graduate students.
1980	Sony Walkman invented. The first mobile phone, known as the AEG Telecar CD, is created.
1981	IBM PC first sold. First laptop computers sold to public. Computer mouse becomes regular part of computer.
1982	The first emoticon is used by Scott Fahlman after a joke :-)

1983	*Time* magazine names the computer as "Man of the Year." First cellular phone network started in the United States.
1984	Domain Name System (DNS) created, making addresses on the Internet more human friendly. Apple Macintosh released. IBM PC AT released. Friedhelm Hillebrand and Bernard Ghillebaert of The Franco-German cooperation (GSM) develop the modern text message.
1985	Virtual Communities; The WELL (Whole Earth 'Lectronic Link) is developed by Stewart Brand and Larry Brilliant and is now one of the oldest virtual communities still in operation. Cellular telephones in cars become widespread. CD-ROMs were used in computers.
1988	First major malicious Internet-based attack. One of the first major Internet worms referred to as "The Morris Worm" was written by Robert Tappan Morris and caused major interruptions.
1989	AOL is launched. The first flip cell phone, the Motorola MicroTAC 9800x, is created. Proposal for the World Wide Web written by Tim Berners-Lee originally published in the March issue of *Macworld*.
1990	First commercial dial-up Internet service provider (ISP) is launched. The first commercial dial-up Internet provider, The World, is launched. ARPANET ceases to exist.

1991	World Wide Web (WWW)
	First web page was created.
	First content-based search protocol; examined file contents instead of just file names, called Gopher.
	MP3 becomes a standard; MP3 files, being highly compressed, later become a popular file format to share songs and entire albums via the Internet.
	The first webcam was deployed at a Cambridge University computer lab, and its sole purpose was to monitor a particular coffee maker so that lab users could avoid wasted trips to an empty coffee pot.
1992	Neil Papworth, a former developer at Sema Group Telecoms, sends the first text message—"Merry Christmas"—to Richard Jarvis at Vodafone.
1993	Mosaic web browser, the first widely downloaded Internet browser, released.
	Governments join in on the fun. The White House and the United Nations came online, marking the beginning of the .gov and .org domain names.
	Nokia becomes the first cell phone manufacturer with a short message service (SMS).
1994	Full text web search engines.
	Phone networks begin offering person-to-person (P2P) SMS text messaging with limited texts per month.
	IBM launches Simon, the world's first "smartphone" with a touchscreen.
	Mosaic's first big competitor, Netscape Navigator, released.

1995	Commercialization of the Internet. The year 1995 is often considered the first year the web became commercialized. Key developments: Secure Sockets Layer (SSL) encryption developed by Netscape, making it safer to conduct financial transactions (like credit card payments) online. Two major online businesses got their start the same year. Echo Bay later became eBay. Amazon.com also started in 1995, though it didn't turn a profit until 2001. The Vatican goes online for the first time. Java and JavaScript (originally called LiveScript by its creator Brendan Eich) deployed as part of the Netscape Navigator browser.
1996	The popular flip phone, the Motorola StarTAC, is created, and it helps start the cell phone craze. First web-based (webmail) service. HoTMaiL (the capitalized letters are an homage to HTML).
1997	Nokia releases the 9000i Communicator, the first cell phone with a full QWERTY keyboard.
1999	Users start exchanging text messages between different networks. Cross-network text messaging makes it possible for everyone to send text messages.
2000	The Sharp J-SHO4 becomes the first cell phone with a camera built in.
2002	The first Blackberry phone.
2003	*American Idol* uses short code text messaging as part of the first "Text to Vote" campaign.
2007	Arrival of Rich Communication Services (RCS). The first iPhone is created by Steve Jobs and Apple. The iPhone allowed for your phone to be an iPod and a telephone, and was able to have games known as "apps."

2010	"Texting" is officially added to the dictionary as a verb.
Examples of popular Internet services	
1990	IMDb Internet movie database. Number of Internet users: 2.6 million.
1994	Number of Internet users: 44.4 million
1995	Microsoft's Internet Explorer launches. Amazon.com online retailer, eBay online auction and shopping, Craigslist classified advertisements launch.
1996	Hotmail free web-based e-mail launches.
1997	Babel Fish automatic translation launches.
1998	Google Search revolutionizes the way in which people find information online.
1999	Napster peer-to-peer file sharing launches.
2000	Number of Internet users: 412.8 million
2001	Wikipedia, the free encyclopedia, launches.
2003	LinkedIn business networking, Myspace social networking site, Skype Internet voice calls, iTunes Store launch.
2004	"Social Media" term believed to be first used by Chris Sharpley. Facebook social networking site, Digg (social news site), Podcast media file series, Flickr image hosting launch.
2005	YouTube video sharing, Google Earth virtual globe launch. Number of Internet users: 1.026 billion
2006	Twitter microblogging launches.

2007	Google Street View came on the scene.
	The iPhone and mobile web was introduced to the public.
	TV shows come online. A joint venture is launched between ABC, NBC and Fox to make popular TV shows available to watch online.
2009	Bing search engine and Bitcoin are introduced.
2010	Instagram & Pinterest are launched, and the iPad is introduced.
	Number of Internet users: 1.992 billion
2011	Snapchat is launched.
2016	Number of Internet users: 3.408 billion
2018	Cambridge Analytica Data scandal.
2019	@world_record_egg account was created with "Let's set a world record together and get the most liked post on Instagram." In less than ten days it beat the previous record held by Kylie Jenner of 18 million. It has since gone on to receive more than fifty million likes.[8, 9, 10, 11, 12]

[8] https://www.visualcapitalist.com/30-year-timeline-world-wide-web/. "The 30 Year History of the World Wide Web," n.d.

[9] https://en.wikipedia.org/wiki/History_of_communication. "History of Communication in Wikipedia," n.d.

[10] https://www.webfx.com/blog/web-design/the-history-of-the-internet-in-a-nutshell/#:~:text=On%20October%20 29%2C%201969%2C%20computers,on%20the%20letter%20 %E2%80%9Cg%E2%80%9D. "History of the Internet in a Nutshell Web FX," n.d.

[11] https://messagedesk.com/blog/text-messaging-history-timeline-evolution/. "MessageDesk; Evolution of Text Messaging and RCS," n.d.

[12] Timetoast.com. "Evolution of the Telephone," n.d.

When phones were tied to wire, humans were free!

As the twentieth century came to an end, communication become more and more about using technology to communicate and less about actual "speaking." Other than postal delivery and the invention of the telephone in 1876 by Alexander Graham Bell, the biggest advancement in communication came in 1995 with the commercialization of the Internet and in 1996 with the first webmail service, Hotmail. Within a matter of twenty years, we increased the speed in which we communicate to a level we could never have imagined. Unlike any other time in history, "time" is of the essence, and we cannot wait even a few hours before responding to a message. Minutes and seconds are the new norm. We can communicate with the world, not just our neighbours and countrymen. Since Facebook and other social media sites are the norm, we can now share our lives, our passions and our idiosyncrasies as, I'm sure, people need to know that the oranges at the local supermarket are the "best ever!"

Nadine F.
Teacher, mother and business owner
Canada

I have been teaching for over twenty years, fifteen of which have been at the kindergarten level. Kids are in school more than they are at home. The good part of technology is we love to keep up with what's going on in society and the world, and since everything is online, we can get our information right away; it's current, happening now. My students can go to YouTube and don't need a million books or encyclopedias for research. The kids can learn at home. There's some great apps out there for learning math and the alphabet, a huge plus. Most older kids have a phone because parents see it as a safety device since the older kids are at home at times after school on their own.

The "bad," and I see this from a mother's perspective, is the peer pressure. There is a need to keep up with the Jones's as far as the devices themselves. Whether it's a phone, tablet or a PC, not all kids can get these devices and they are not part of the "in crowd" if they don't have the newest phone or device.

We also see that these devices are good babysitters, and parents do say that they limit the screen time. However, it is a chance for them to get other things done when their kids are online. My observation in my kindergarten class is what tools the kids are not using. They need more occupational therapists because they don't colour, write and do crafts anymore, we need to show them how to hold a pencil or a pair of scissors. This is happening more now than in the past when I first started teaching.

In the general school population, not necessarily in my kindergarten class, kids are losing the ability to communicate. Since they are not communicating face to face as much as they used to, they are losing those social cues and body language indications. When they get face to face, they don't know how to read those cues and so they are losing that social connection. They are hiding behind a screen.

Personally, I see for the future that we won't be able to do anything anymore without our devices or without using the Internet, its where we are going. It's a fast-paced path we are on and we can't get off, we need to keep up with everyone else. If we want to know what's going in China, we just click and the information is there immediately. I am also a business owner so I find it's absolutely necessary.

As a woman, I do see that teen girls' social skills suffer. They need that instant gratification and want to see right away if their post was liked or why they didn't get a response to their post right away—what's going on? The photo that they just posted a minute ago, (and they take quite a few photos to get the best one), is now out there for all to see, they are now waiting to see if someone likes the way they looked. The stress and anxiety that comes with this is immense, especially the girls, that need to feel empowered, its controlling how they feel about themselves. The phone tells you if you are good or not. The apps that the girls use to filter the face distort reality. In the past magazines influenced us as girls, the photo edits of the beautiful cover models was a slightly unreal representation of the real thing now with technology, girls can edit themselves and these filters are amazing, they change the face completely. It's totally unreal.

We have a rule at the supper table: "No phones, no books, no TV. It's time to talk, no distractions." My husband and I have always had that rule, so we tell our kids, "Put your phones away, you can wait." When I'm with a friend, I put my phone away, otherwise we are losing that human contact. If we have someone right in front of us, we need to give them our full attention.

Nadine has seen first-hand how students and school have changed throughout more than twenty years in teaching. If a kindergartner has to learn how to use a pencil, crayons or scissors will they lose the ability to use their hands for other simple tasks that require dexterity. Will they be able to create an amazing piece of art on a canvas, or will that soon become a lost skill? A teen girl who might already be suffering from the usual teen angst has to deal with being "liked" on many different levels. They also are wanting to achieve that attention with a distorted view of themselves by using apps and filters to change the way they look then posting online as the 'real me'. In fact, it is always about "Me." The selfies and the constant attention to themselves leads to high expectations that don't match reality. This begs us to wonder how this will help with their confidence. Does this support the rise in depression and anxiety among teens today?

It's enlightening to see how far we have come from hieroglyphic writing, homing pigeons and human messengers. Some questions to think about:

- At the speed we are going, how can we keep up with technology when it's coming at us from everywhere?
- When can we take a break and "get off the fast train" before we hit the speed of light and not know where we are?
- At some point, will we lose the ability to speak since we won't need our voice box and evolution will have its way?

Many developing countries still operate on a simpler system of communication and are certainly not at the level the developed world operates at. This digital divide challenges these countries to compete in this fast-paced tech world, so they may be at a disadvantage. Or will they survive an evolutionary shift while the rest of us gain strides technically but lose the ability to speak and suffer with disconnection on a human level? If the developed world suffers a major computer crash with widespread financial ruin and no way to communicate electronically, will we remember how to communicate without e-mail, messaging and social media? It may be a far-fetched or silly concept to think about, but the Internet is like food or water: we cannot function without it. If it all went down tomorrow, what would we do?

A question for you:

If there was a power outage and therefore no phone reception and no Internet for the day, what would you do all day? How would you communicate?

If history has taught us one thing, it's that change is constant. It is expected, of course, and part of our evolution, however, there has to be a balance that allows us to evolve but not lose our humanity. We need to remember how we got here and how it can be gone in a flash. For example, a pandemic can bring us back to reality, a reality where we missed those one-on-one conversations, physically hugging our loved ones and being able to see a facial expression without a mask. It was clear to us, during a lockdown, that we need human to human interaction, we need a personal touch, that eye contact and a real smile to feel more 'human'. We are not happy when we isolate and can only communicate via a text message; it just doesn't do it for us. As Daft Punk would say, we are "human after all"![13]

---

[13] "Daft Punk 'Human After All'." Human After All, n.d.

Play the "What if?" Game

Want some interesting no-tech conversation at the dinner table? Play the "What if?" game. It's a great way to see how good you are at problem-solving.

What if:

    a. The Internet went down
- Read a book, play a game, go for a walk

    b. You couldn't use your phone to find where you're going
- Get a map

    c. You couldn't pay your bills online
- Call them, go to the bank

    d. You couldn't wish a happy birthday on social media
- Call and actually speak with them, meet with them and give them a hug. If time permits, send them an actual birthday card in the mail

    e. The power goes down and the lights go out
- Light a candle and tell spooky stories

In the next chapter, we will explore the statistics, facts and figures that show how we communicate today.

Will the statistics surprise you?

If they don't surprise you, maybe that's the problem. We've become complacent and accepted what seems inevitable. Maybe we've thrown up our hands and said, "What can we do?"

CHAPTER THREE

How Do We Communicate Today?

Wise men speak because they have something to say; fools because they have to say something.

Plato

E-mail, A Personal Story

To me, e-mail is similar to sending a personal note or letter to another individual, from my computer to theirs. Since this is one of the first ways I used to connect electronically, back when e-mail was in its infancy, this is the one I prefer to use on a regular basis. It's the one I know and understand the best. I know who I am sending the message to without worrying that others may see it in an open forum (like on social media). Although you can also send personal messages via social networking, I feel safer using e-mail. With all my file folders, contacts list and sorting abilities, I rely on e-mail for all my online personal and business communication.

Enter my new iPhone. For a long time, I had a basic cell phone with no access to the Internet and, therefore, no access my e-mail. It was time to ditch the old cell and leap into the new world of access anytime, anywhere. At first it was liberating. I could check my e-mail while waiting for a doctor's appointment, in line at the grocery store or when I was getting my hair done. It was instant, immediate, and I could reply within seconds.

It was a double-edged sword, though. Friends, family and business associates began to expect that immediate reply, and when they didn't get a response right away, they often wondered where I was or what happened. This never happened in the past. If I hadn't checked my e-mail, I was either in the car or simply at home relaxing after a long day of work. I never stressed about my e-mail messages because I wasn't at work or on my PC. Family would call if they needed to get a hold of me after the workday.

Enter my iPhone addiction. Having access at anytime, anywhere was addictive. I was checking my e-mail in bed before I went to sleep and again when I woke up. My iPhone was the first thing I reached for, probably because I set my alarm on it. I would instantly be brought to attention at the sound of the ping and the following vibrating echo that the phone would make when sitting on my bedside table or the kitchen counter. I was taking it into the washroom and left it beside me while I was getting ready in the morning. I would take it into the kitchen while I was cooking and even looked up a few recipes while I had the chicken in the oven. I could check the temperature outside, listen to the music I downloaded, check the map app to see where I needed to go for a meeting, peruse my calendar to see what was on for the day, build my to-do list (yes, I need to pick up orange juice) and even watch my morning news show on a screen no larger than the palm of my hand. I didn't need anything else. No scraps of paper with reminders, no turning on the TV, no GPS. All I needed with me at all times was this pink polka-dotted mini PC.

I discovered I was addicted when I was sending an e-mail while at the movie theatre with my husband and our son. I looked over at another mother, also frantically typing into her iPhone, and I realized we were one and the same. Obviously, whatever we were communicating had to be so urgent that we couldn't wait until we got home. No, it had to be done here and now while we were out for some rare family time. Why? Because we could.

I was becoming exactly like the people I so often chastised under my breath. Husbands and wives out for a nice dinner, one on the phone talking, the other texting. Families out together; mums, dads, and kids hunched over their devices completely engrossed with whatever they were reading and not interacting with each other. They were interacting with someone else, playing a game, checking Facebook, searching the Internet—anything other than connecting with the loved ones around the table.

In 2018, a teenager's favourite way to communicate with friends was via text. In fact, a study from Common Sense Media[14] compared how teens communicated with friends in 2012 to how they communicated in 2018. "In-person" communication fell from 49 percent to 32 percent. Texting, social media and video chatting all increased over the time period. A further study was conducted in 2020, and the texting statistic rose to 83 percent. The numbers were no doubt impacted by the COVID-19 pandemic, however, it shows that texting is becoming the main form of communication between teens. Thus, talking, actually speaking real words, is becoming a rarity amongst our youth.

Think about the kids sitting on a bench in the mall. They could have a conversation with each other, but they are texting each other instead. Yes, they are sitting knee to knee but would rather communicate electronically than in person. Just the other day I was in a restaurant with my family. Another family of five were out together for a meal, and all of them were on their phones talking or texting; I see this often. The only one not participating electronically was the youngest, who looked about five. He was playing "airplane" by himself with his fork. Were there urgent messages they all had to attend to? Possibly. Or was it quality family time wasted?

How difficult is it to get your kids off the Internet or away from their favourite video game? I don't know how many times I have called my son down for supper only to get the usual, "I'll be there in a minute, just finishing this mission." I have lost count of how many times I have asked my husband to join me for a walk with the dog without his phone. "What if I need it for an emergency?"

---

[14]   https://www.commonsensemedia.org/press-releases/common-sense-research-reveals-everything-you-need-to-know-about-teens-use-of-social-media-in-2018. "Less Talk More Texting, Common Sense Media," n.d.

is the usual answer. I'm pretty sure we won't get mugged going around the block, Honey!

The thing is, we all have a problem putting down our devices, logging off the Internet and checking that one last e-mail. We can access anything anywhere at any time and it's addictive. Even my mother, who is attached at the hip to her iPad, loves to look things up online when we are just chatting over a cup of tea. That irritating *ping* signals an immediate halt to our conversation because the e-mail or text just might be something important. Ninety-nine percent of the time it isn't.

A survey of six thousand business travellers by Four Points Sheraton hotels found that we put a higher priority on our e-mail than our families. Asked what they do when they wake up, 36 percent of people surveyed said they check their smartphones, 19 percent said they turn on the TV. Take a shower was at 18 percent, and checking Twitter and calling home was tied for fifth place at 7 percent.[15] If we did similar a survey today would the statistics increase?

What is the first thing you do when you wake up? Do you grab your smartphone from your bedside table and go online to start your day? How much time do we spend online? Do we think it's a problem? Are our kids addicted to being online, texting, the Internet, gaming or social media? Let's look at some statistics that might shock you.

---

[15] https://www.businesswire.com/news/home/20120820005084/en/ Four-Points-by-Sheraton-Survey-Reveals-Mobile-Device-Habits-of-Business-Travellers-Worldwide. "Breaking Travel News.Com; News Article, Four Points by Sheraton Survey Reveals Mobile Device Habits," n.d.

A few years ago, a *Readers Digest/* Yahoo poll found the following:

- The number of digital devices in an average household: 20.
- 43 percent of adults think they spend too much time online.
- 64 percent of adults think kids spend too much time online.
- Adults spend an average of five hours online at home every day.
- One in sixteen kids under age five has a Facebook page.
- 78 percent of kids surveyed have stayed up past their bedtime because they are online.
- Average number of mobile phones per household: 3.

These statistics were surprising and certainly gave me food for thought, however, these statistics pale in comparison to what was to come. A more recent study by Common Sense Media looked at kids under the age of eight and the statistics are alarming.[16]

- In 2011, only 41 percent of families had a mobile device; now 95 percent do.
- In 2011, less than 10 percent of families had a tablet; now nearly 80 percent do.
- For kids under the age of eight, the average amount of time spent with mobile devices each day has tripled, going from five minutes per day in 2011, fifteen minutes per day in 2013, and forty-eight minutes per day in 2017.

---

[16] https://www.commonsensemedia.org/sites/default/files/research/report/2020_zero_to_eight_census_final_web.pdf. "The Common Sense Census: Media Use by Kids Age Zero to Eight," n.d.

What about Texting?

Texting has become a popular way of communicating because it's a fast, easy way to get the info to your partner, best friend or boss. However, many teens text more than sixty messages a day, and one in three teens send more than one hundred texts a day. That's three thousand texts a month,[17] and some studies suggest as high as ten thousand texts each month.

So, what are they texting?

Let's face it: 50 percent are usually about scoring a great sweater or taking the dog for a walk, but they can also be about alcohol, drugs and crime. Parents know that kids do not go from perfect angel to consuming hard drugs overnight, nor do they decide to engage in high-risk behaviours instantly. Instead, there are a series of choices made and steps taken that lead to life-altering—or even life-ending—behaviour. For the parents who want to take the next step to help their kids make the right choices early on, monitoring your kids' text messaging is key. Apps like Spyic or Webwatcher work well.[18]

Harassment, bullying, sexting, and texting while driving are all realities of most teens' daily lives, but I'm also concerned about the fact that there is little communication other than texting. Texting has overtaken every other common form of interaction with their friends (Pew Research Center). All this is communicated via a device and behind the scenes where it's more difficult to see the signs.

[17] https://www.pewresearch.org/internet/2012/03/19/teens-smartphones-texting/. "Pew Research Center Teens Smart Phones and Texting," n.d.
[18] Wondershare https://famisafe.wondershare.com/child-monitoring/how-can-i-monitor-my-childs-text-messages.html. "Wondershare," n.d.

Some more interesting statistics:[19]

- The number of monthly texts sent increased more than 7,700 percent over the last decade. (Statistic Brain)
- Over 560 billion texts are sent every month worldwide. (Statistic Brain)
- 18.7 billion texts are sent worldwide every day, not including app-to-app messaging. (Statistic Brain)
- Text messaging is the most used data service in the world. (Nielsen)
- 91 percent of teens with cell phones actively text. (Pew Research Center)
- About 50 percent of adults between the ages of eighteen and twenty-four say text conversations as just as meaningful as a phone call. (Experian Marketing Services)
- Adults under forty-five send and receive more than eighty-five texts every day on average. (Experian Marketing Services)
- Adults between the ages of eighteen and twenty-four send and receive over 128 texts every day. (Experian Marketing Services)
- 55 percent of heavy text message users (more than fifty texts per day) say they would prefer to receive a text over a phone call. (Pew Research Center)

Do these statistics surprise you? Some of are a little outdated, so new research may show even more alarming results. Maybe they don't surprise you, but maybe that's the problem. We are accustomed to this and have become complacent. Maybe we are just as guilty as our kids when it comes to time on our phones!

---

[19] https://shso.vermont.gov/sites/ghsp/files/documents/Worldwide%20 Texting%20Statistics.pdf. "Worldwide Texting Statistics," n.d.

Sleep Texting on the Rise[20]

New research in the US has found that sleep texting—using smartphones late at night to message friends—is on the rise amongst teens and college students.

Carried out by researchers at Villanova University's M. Louise Fitzpatrick College of Nursing, the new study recruited 372 college students and surveyed them about their cell phone use during sleep as well as the location of their phone at night, their sleep quality and the number of hours of sleep they get on a school night and over the weekend.

The findings, published in the *Journal of American College Health*, showed that 25.6 percent of the students reported texting in their sleep, poor sleep quality, and that their cell phone influences their sleep. Of these students, 72 percent also reported that they do not remember sleep texting, and 25 percent failed to remember what they had texted.

What about Social Networking?

If you're not aware of this, you've probably been living on another planet, but social networking has totally changed the way people communicate and share information. There are entire books devoted to the social network phenomenon so I won't delve into

---

[20] CTV News. "'Sleep Texting' on the Rise among Teenagers: Study." https://www.ctvnews.ca/health/sleep-texting-on-the-rise-among-teenagers-study-1.4196063?cache=lxaherxk, n.d.

detail here, however, I thought it would be interesting to look at the most recent statistics:[21]

- Total number of active users worldwide (2021)
  - Facebook: 2.8 billion
  - YouTube: 2.2 billion
  - Instagram: 1.3 billion
  - Twitter: 436 million

- Social media usage is one of the most popular online activities. In 2020, over 3.6 billion people were using social media worldwide, a number projected to increase to almost 4.41 billion in 2025.

- Social media is an integral part of daily Internet usage. On average, Internet users spend 144 minutes per day on social media and messaging apps, an increase of more than half an hour since 2015. Internet users in Latin America had the highest average time spent per day on social media.

What is it about social networking that has everyone using it? Research and basic observation points to the fact that it lets us stay in touch with family members and connect with friends locally and globally. We know about each other's hobbies and interests, we know what products they like, and we love those inspiring quotes and entertaining videos. Social media is great for keeping in contact with a lot of people at the same time, and it's "free."

This all sounds great because we all need to stay connected. However, what about celebrations? When a close family member is celebrating a major milestone in their life, is a Facebook post the best way to connect and share in their big day? Have we eliminated the gesture of a phone call or a card? What about when a loved one

---

[21] https://datareportal.com/social-media-users. "Most Popular Social Networks Worldwide," n.d.

passes? Is a "Sorry for your loss" post the best way to extend your true condolences? Maybe for a friend, but for a family member?

As I am writing this book, the world is opening up after the COVID-19 pandemic. We are feeling more isolated than ever before and there seems to be a general feeling that we need to reconnect in a real way, person to person in a one-on-one conversation. For so long during the pandemic it seemed to be a rarity and one that will, and needs, to come back into the limelight.

Let's face it: texting is the easy way out. Why call someone to ask them how their date went when you can just text them? It saves time and you won't get into a lengthy conversation that you simply don't have time for. Maybe that's it: "time"? Or maybe people just don't possess the communication and listening skills to engage in a real conversation anymore. Are we uncomfortable talking about "real" issues and challenges and simply don't know what to say? Maybe people just like to share everything and anything because they are lonely and in need of attention and social networking is a way to get the message out to anyone who is willing to listen.

Texting and messaging seem pretty effortless because they're accessible using the devices we always have with us. Phones are not really phones anymore; we use them for pretty much everything.

Think about why you use social networking—the real reason why. Think about what it would mean to someone if you picked up the phone and actually called them, especially someone who may need a real friend who is willing to spend the time with them and really listen.

Colin Beaton
Architect
Dubai, UAE

Over the last ten years, texting, messaging and technology in general has affected me and my work mostly in a negative way. I think it has complicated my life as I have many more types, formats and channels of communication to manage, and there is a much larger amount of information to manage and process. I believe that a lot of the information now tends to be unnecessary, superfluous, poorly considered, useless or blatant marketing and sales, and there is very little ability to filter it out. The immediacy of social media creates the perception that you can demand an immediate response, and the role of civility and manners seems to have diminished in our daily lives. More is not always better, sometimes it's just more.

On a positive note as far as my personal life is concerned, social media has helped the relationship with my daughter (twenty-six) and family. I live 10,000 kilometres away, so communications with my family is always a priority. I was satisfied to a large degree with a phone call, but video calls are much better. They enable smaller, more frequent interactions rather than long periods of time on long, expensive phone calls. All my family appreciates everyone being in on one conversation. Contact with my family is the biggest benefit for me from social media.

However, our attachment to social media and our devices has an overall negative effect:

1. It provides the crazies and nutjobs a global audience for lies and propaganda (hence the rise of the alt-right).
2. The obsession with beauty and glamour is bad for young women.
3. It's a 24/7 experience that many people can't turn off.

4.   The fixation on popularity and exposure provides a false sense of self-worth.
5.   People are focused on the digital world and fail to live in the moment with the people they love (and who love them) who are physically near.

In general, I'm moderately negative about social media. I understand the benefits and use it all the time, but that doesn't mean I like it. I could easily live without it. I regularly turn off my phone for days to disengage. I think social media has caused quite a bit of harm to our society and culture.

As a busy architect in a key financial and trading hub like Dubai, Colin recognizes that being connected is essential for business purposes, but has its downside. It is also interesting to note that as an Islamic state, visitors to Dubai are expected to comply with local cultural norms or risk the consequences. Swearing in public or use of offensive gestures for example can land you in jail, yet this is often the norm online.

What about Online Video Games?

Another way we communicate is through online gaming.

My son has an xBox, a PlayStation 3, a PlayStation 4, a Wii, a gaming PC, and now the new HTC Vive virtual reality system. His life, from the age of about nine to fifteen, revolved around video games. For the longest time I felt that this was a real big deal and would affect his future drastically. I was sure his brain was going to be filled with violent images which would affect his behaviour. I figured his eyesight was surely going to be affected and he would develop carpal tunnel syndrome. Because he was spending so much time in his room, it could only mean he was to become antisocial, depressed and possibly even a suicidal young man. I am a mother and therefore a worrier—it goes with the territory—so I dove into the research to find all the evidence I could to prove that video games would eventually rot my son's brain. Some statistics I came across were alarming, however, I found some great websites with real solutions. To my surprise, not all of what I found was negative; I have to admit I agree with the positives and have seen this first-hand with my son (more on that in Chapter 5).

The statistics:[22]

- 41 percent of people who play online video games admitted that they played computer games as an escape from the real world. Addicted gamers used video games to modify their moods. Hussain (2009)

- Students addicted to video games have lower academic grades than their non-addicted peers. Chiu (2004)

- In a German sample, 1.5 to 3.5 percent of teens who use the Internet demonstrated symptoms of video game addiction. Video game addiction was also correlated with a higher probability of depression, anxiety and poorer school grades. Peukert (2010)

- Online role-playing games (especially multiplayer games or MMOs) are more likely to result in video game addiction than other computer game genres. Van Rooij (2010)

- Video game addicts may play online role-playing games to avoid or distract themselves from negative moods. Hussain (2009)

---

[22] http://www.techaddiction.ca/video_game_addiction_statistics.html. "Video Game Addiction Statistics," n.d.

- Males are more likely to play online video games. Male video game addicts are more likely to be older, have lower self-esteem and be less satisfied with their lives compared to those who are not addicted. Ko (2005)

Serena Fyvie, BA
Creative Producer (Theatre and Short Film) Program/
Mature Student & Business Support Officer
UK

I've only had an Android phone since August 2017. I was happy with a basic mobile that I used mainly for calls, texting and emergencies, but when I had to move locations, I found it easier to upgrade it to include the Internet so I was not offline during my move and whilst looking for work.

Now I use my mobile to make calls, text, surf the Internet, maintain my calendar, set my alarm clock, do a little online shopping, plan trips, check the weather and communicate on WhatsApp and Messenger.

What I like about having all this access is that it makes it easier to keep in touch with friends and family, travel and leave messages for people, especially if plans change at the last minute. I get Google Maps and directions on my phone, so it was great when I moved or when I was going somewhere new.

Mobile packages for calls, texting and data are getting cheaper. I am not currently connected to the Internet at home, nor do I have a landline, but I'm working on it. I have a dongle (adapter) for connecting my laptop to the Internet, but with limited data.

It's great having WhatsApp for individual and group conversations to share pictures and documents, and having the Internet on my phone is excellent for studying and research. Plus, if I need help covering an out-of-hours shift at work, someone will usually respond quickly.

While I get the need for being connected 24/7 is there, I find that people expect you to have an "all messaging and Internet" phone these days and be always contactable—that includes work. I think

I have too many WhatsApp groups for university and work. I have struggled at university as a mature student moving from a work environment with Microsoft business packages to university where technology set up and software packages are more familiar to younger students who are familiar with online games and apps. Some university groups include teachers. If I don't respond straight away to a message, some people take offence. Students seem to prefer to set up a group on WhatsApp or Messenger for tasks rather than meet face to face. I have experienced fellow students being uncomfortable in even a small group environment and stating that they have anxiety issues or don't feel comfortable doing group work outside of formal lessons. Whilst consideration and assistance is there to support anxiety and mental health, I do not believe society is helping build resilience when allowing people to rely on mobile communications and opting out of face-to-face situations.

I find it very irritating when I'm in a social environment and people are using mobile phones rather than talking to the people they're with.

Working in volunteer and community groups over the past ten years, I have seen issues relating to loneliness, isolation and mental health on the increase even though social media connects people. My oldest sister sent me a text message to inform me of the arrangements for my mother's funeral. A long and sad story of how a sibling's revenge can be aided by hiding behind technology.

Technology has helped me organize myself and keep in touch with friends and family all over the world, but making new friends or building new relationships, especially in the last ten years, has been very difficult because I don't feel comfortable with how technology seems to govern the dynamics of personal relationships. And I don't like being made to feel I should be constantly available.

It's very sad to think that keeping up with technology is seen as a necessity. I think social skills and etiquette are on the decline, along with the art of conversation. I am appalled when I see "text speak" in business communications. Acceptance in the forms of likes and followers on social media seems to be more important to younger generations than engaging in face-to-face interaction.

Turning off, spending time on my own or in nature is something I need for my well-being, but this seems to be out of fashion! It saddens me to think of a future with a population reliant on technology who only do things for someone else if they can be promoted to and liked by the unknown masses.

The thought that technology is more important than personal human contact scares me not just for myself, but for the future of humankind

Serena is experiencing what many of us are: that need for everyone to communicate via technology even when we should probably meet or at least talk on the phone. Where did personal concern and etiquette go? Are we distancing and separating ourselves from other humans because we've lost the ability to connect in person? It is so much easier to send a text or post a message, but should we?

Is this how we communicate in modern day society?:[23]

- E-mails instead of letters
- Little thought involved when writing so you write something off the top of your head and then regret what you wrote and wish you had an undo button
- Using the phone for just about everything
- You update your Facebook page instead of contacting people directly
- Etiquette? Just good manners have changed; we snoop on other's private lives online
- Families are divided. Everybody in the family has a TV, computer and/or video game in their own room and so families lead separate lives rather than gathering together
- We are at the beck and call of our servants: the phone and computer
- We answer the phone when it rings and ignore the people we're with, which makes us rude and discourteous
- Anything anybody wants to say they can say to everybody without real repercussions
- We live locked in our own little worlds. We shut out the outside world by talking on our cell phones and putting our earbuds in
- We connect with people everywhere and rarely, if ever, see them in person
- We ignore the people next to us in favour of people far away

---

[23] https://public.wsu.edu/~taflinge/com101/Outlines/ MODERNCOMMUNICATIONANDSOCIETY.html. "Modern Communication and Society," n.d.

Maybe some of these statements ring true for you?

Here's some questions.

- How do you communicate on a daily basis?
- Have you tracked how much time you spend on your phone, PC, social media?
- Are you speaking less and typing more?

Thinking back to my personal e-mail story at the beginning of this chapter, I have since become more aware of my own habits and decided to break my addiction, to cut the umbilical cord and find my way back to communicating the right way (a topic I cover in Chapter 6: "Bringing Back the Art of Conversation"). But before we get there, we need to look at the effects that our addiction is having on us and society. Do you want the good news or the bad news first? Let's start with the good news because I want to be clear that it's not all bad.

CHAPTER FOUR

The Good.
It's not all bad

*I'm a great believer that any tool that enhances communication
has profound effects in terms of how people can learn from each
other and how they can achieve the kind of freedoms that they're
interested in.*

Bill Gates

Virtual communication has impacted our daily lives dramatically.

What do we do as soon as we wake up? Many of us keep our phones right beside our beds and, like many others, I use mine for the alarm. When the alarm goes off, I might notice that I had a text message (sent after we went to sleep) inviting me to a friend's birthday party. I open this text message and there is a link to the Facebook invite where I see who else has been invited and who has RSVP'd. While on Facebook I see that my sister posted pictures of her vacation, so I "like" the post and then notice a really cool dog stunt video I wanted to watch. Twenty minutes later, I realize I haven't even brushed my teeth! The good news is that I was able to do all this in a mere twenty minutes, the bad news is that I took twenty minutes to do something that could have been done later. Now I'm late for work.

As with everything in life, we have the good and the bad. And because life likes to make things interesting, we can get the downright ugly. In this chapter, we will look at how virtual communication impacts our lives and those around us for the good.

Jacqueline Green, BA
Founder of the Great Parenting Simplified movement
Canada

Growing up, we had a big advantage of being able to live more of our time away from peer influences. That meant that when we left school for the day, most of us had much more of a break from peer pressures. That made our peers a bit less important, which made it easier for us to pursue hobbies without worrying about what was cool or popular to do.

Our parents also weren't as influenced by what other parents were doing. That helped them to be more confident, which often created a healthier climate for their children; nowadays, parents are often anxious and full of doubts about whether they are doing it "right."

However, there are positives for parents and children. We are often able to get help more easily online than in the past where our options for finding help were more limited. As well, we can stay connected to friends and family in a way that was not possible before. That's enabled our children to be supported by people whom they don't see often.

My kids are adults, and it is still relevant, as they have seen me display good boundaries. I am not constantly on my phone. When we are together, I have the phone away for most of the time. I barely watch TV, so neither of them got in the habit either. I do sometimes debate taking more vacations without my phone!

Often when parents are feeling stressed, they reach for their phones to distract them, just like any addictive behaviours. Parenting is much harder than ever before, hence why parents are more stressed and wanting an escape. It's important to understand this dynamic so that we don't shame parents and they don't shame themselves. That only adds stress and can lead to increasing the drive to be on their phones. I'm passionate about helping the parents I work closely with to learn to reduce their stress, which helps them to model good behaviour for their kids.

Technology can be good, but when we come from a place of fear about technology, our kids will resist us. We can use technology as a friend to help us to connect with extended family and friends.

Jacqueline has found a happy medium when using technology and shares her approach with parents. Technology is here to stay—we are not going to eliminate it—so we must recognize what it can and can't do for our lives, especially when we are setting the example for our children.

Our communication methods can't all be bad, right? There must be some advantages to being able to communicate within seconds, have a device at our fingertips to access anything, anytime, anywhere and all without having to utter a single word to another human being. Here are a few "good" areas we must remember. Advancement and evolution is inevitable, and change is good if used appropriately. Here are just a few of the "goods"!

Increased Security

Our homes are safer with our camera at our front door, our automated door locks and our controlled lighting that we can access from our phone. We are connected to our kids and our loved ones in case of emergency, and we can call 911 in seconds if needed. If you have a weird bump on your neck, you can look up "weird bump on my neck" to see what it might be. Is it an enlarged lymph node (probably!) or a tumour (unlikely!)?

Improved Health

Speaking of those weird bumps, we can monitor our heart rate, weight and a host of other health options from our phone. Most hospitals have made big improvements in healthcare technology, and doctors today can communicate and share information with patients and colleagues around the world faster and easier.

Amazing Entertainment

We are not prisoners to our TVs anymore. Music, TV shows and movies are all available at our fingertips anytime, anywhere. We can watch past episodes of our favourite shows or create playlists of our favourite music as well as numerous other customized options.

Stunning Photography

Feel like taking a photo of the strange looking melon at the grocery store? Go ahead! Then send it to you brother who just said that his head looks like a melon. No more paying for printed photos anymore either; we can share them easily with friends and family.

Enhanced Skills and Education

We have access to huge amounts of information which makes homework so much easier for students. We also have access to online courses that we can take at our convenience, submit homework and interact with fellow students and teachers in chat rooms or online forums.

Many courses are free, which allows everyone the opportunity to learn something new whether it's how to change a tire, speak Spanish or negotiate a contract. Plus, kids are getting a head start at school using apps and games that teach them basic math or reading. Even video games require manual dexterity and may help hand-eye coordination; kids become familiar with technology at an early age. Companies like Spongelab[24] are developing educational games like *Transcription Hero*, which uses a *Guitar Hero*-style controller to allow kids to sequence DNA.

 ## Are Video Games Harmful to the Eyes?

Video games sharpen your child's vision and strengthen:

- eye movement skills: being able to move your eyes in all directions smoothly
- hand-eye coordination: simultaneous hand and eye movement
- visual reaction times: the time required to react to visual cues

Dr. Sean Moir, an optometrist who practises in Alberta, Canada, says that a recent study at McGill University[25] in Montreal showed that playing *Tetris* can actually have positive benefits for amblyopia, a condition commonly referred to as "lazy eye" (when one eye does not develop properly and does not work with the other eye). *Tetris* has been found to force both eyes to work together. An estimated one in fifty children are diagnosed with amblyopia. Moderation is key, however. Monitor time spent on gaming, keep at least five feet from the screen and take regular breaks.

---

24   https://www.spongelab.com/game_pages/transcription_hero.cfm. "Spongelab," n.d.

25   https://www.mcgill.ca/newsroom/channels/news/lazy-eye-disorder-promising-therapeutic-approach-226011. "McGill University Study," n.d.

Get Off Your Butt and Go Outside!

Back in 2012, concerned Children's' Advertisers, (renamed to Companies Committed to Kids, a non-profit originally founded in 1990) brought technology and exercise together to harness the allure of online gaming as an incentive to get kids moving. Each child's daily exercise is measured by a Fitbit that's worn all day then uploaded to a PC. This exercise becomes the sole source of power for a game called Gogoyu.[26] Don't want to go out and play? Then you can't earn the steps you need to log on. In Gogoyu, kids create their own avatar that uses their steps to travel the world with the ultimate goal of reaching the moon.

There are also video game series that include dance and rock bands, and with the virtual reality craze, there are many options for combining movement and fitness. My son is a huge Beat Saber[27] fan and ranks highly nationally and globally; he has amazing upper body strength.

Clearer Communication

Today, distance is not an obstacle. We can just as easily send a message to someone sitting right next to us as we can across the globe. We can do it via social media, e-mail, videos, blogs, forums, video conferencing and texting. We can communicate with one person or thousands of people. Communication today speeds things up so we can be more productive. Need an answer ASAP? You'll probably get it.

---

[26] https://www.youtube.com/watch?v=j2bOVr2jE48. "Gogoyu," n.d.

[27] https://beatsaber.com/. "Beat Saber," n.d.

Ubiquitous Apps

The total number of mobile apps downloaded worldwide in 2020 was 230 billion, and it is still rising.[28] The app (short for application) is a type of software that can be installed and run on a computer, tablet, smartphone or other electronic devices. Everyone has an app of some type. If you've ever heard the phrase, "There's an app for that," it is true. There's an app for just about anything you could ever want to do on your phone or tablet in various categories like business, productivity, shopping and scheduling. They are easy to access, simple to use. If you own a business, the benefits of having an app are numerous, especially if you want to raise awareness about your products and communicate the values of your brand.

 Parent Control Apps Keep Your Kids Safe on Their Devices

Are your kids constantly on TikTok, Snapchat or Facebook Messenger? Do they quickly hide their phone when you walk into the room? What are they doing that they need to hide from you?

Parental control apps for smartphones and tablets help you keep an eye on what your kids are doing in cyberspace and in the physical world. Apps like Net Nanny[29] can:

- Show you who they are communicating with
- Block apps and websites
- Filter adult content and block pornography
- Set limits on their daily screen time and send alerts of online activity

---

[28]   https://www.statista.com/topics/1002/mobile-app-usage/. "Mobile App Usage," n.d.

[29]   https://www.netnanny.com/. "Net Nanny," n.d.

- Track their physical location with GPS

And much more.

An app can only do so much, of course, so we still need to teach our kids what they should and shouldn't do online. However, if they know we will be monitoring their devices, they may behave more responsibly.

The Virtual Office

The traditional workplace is changing. Gone are the days when we must fight traffic and bad weather to get into work. For many employees, working from home is the new norm, and many forward-thinking companies are realizing that the team doesn't have to be in the office to be productive. There is a shift towards companies offering telecommuting as a perk, and it's doable because of largely free and user-friendly web-based project management and communication tools like Zoom, Webex, Microsoft Teams and GoTo Meeting for web conferences.

The COVID-19 pandemic changed the way people work. A recent Global Workplace Analytics study in the US found:[30]

- 56 percent of employees have a job where at least some of what they do could be done remotely
- 82 percent of employees reported wanting to work remotely at least once a week after the COVID-19 pandemic ended.

Global Workplace Analytics estimates a typical US employer can save an average of $11,000 per half-time telecommuter per year.

---

[30] https://globalworkplaceanalytics.com/telecommuting-statistics. "Global Workplace Analytics," n.d.

So we can save money on babysitting costs, gas, eating out and still get that load of laundry done while we work away in our home office!

Social Networking and Media

What did we do without Facebook twenty years ago? First of all, it's one of the best ways to stay informed. Earthquake in Hawaii? Protest in Paris? We will hear about it as soon as it reaches the airwaves or the Internet. And if a natural disaster hits close to home, we'll know immediately and even get an emergency alert text! From a business perspective, Facebook is the most cost-effective way to reach a mass number of consumers. Consumers that support a cause, product or service are more likely to share posts from major corporations and non-profit organizations.

Social media can build relationships whether in a group setting where there are shared interests or on a personal level with family and friends.

Grandma Is on Facebook

Who gets the award for the fastest growing age group on social media? Seniors. Some interesting statistics from a Pew Research Center report (2019)[31] found that 69 percent of adults between the ages of fifty and sixty-four and 40 percent of those above sixty-five use social media. Forty-one percent of Facebook users are over the age of sixty-five.

More seniors have smartphones and tablets today (and all the apps that are included). They are adopting tools like Skype and Zoom as well as streaming services like Netflix. They're engaging in

---

[31]   https://www.pewresearch.org/internet/fact-sheet/social-media/. "Pew Research Center Fact Sheet," n.d.

telehealth doctor visits and monitoring their health with Fitbits and Apple watches.

Why do you think this is? Because they want to connect with their friends and family more easily, it alleviates the loneliness that they often experience, and they don't have to get out of their easy chair. My mother doesn't go anywhere without her phone or tablet as she's usually waiting for a video of a grandchild or a message from her sister.

Internet Banking

More and more of us are switching to online banking. Not only can we pay bills and move our money as we see fit, but we can also now e-transfer money to our sister for that gift we agreed to go in for. Those inconvenient trips to the bank to wait in a long line to withdraw or deposit OUR money are over.

Search It

We all have heard the phrase, "Just search it on the Internet." There isn't anything out there that I have searched for and not be able to find via a search engine. Literally, you can search for anything, and I think we often forget that this is an amazing thing to be able to do. Whether you are searching for "red owls with blue eyes" or "the Chinese art of face reading," you will find it on the Internet!

Technology has created some pretty fantastic ways to enhance our lives and make things easier. Many of us can't remember our lives without Google, Facebook or being able to watch a movie on our phone. We have never been able to take as much control as can now. We need less and less help. We can do it all ourselves, and this leaves us more and more isolated. Independence is great, yet we are still engaging with a device. The questions are: When does it stop? How do we escape the constant onslaught of communication and information without speaking in person to any other human? Where do we draw the line?

Communicating through technology simply makes things so much easier, and we love that. Muhammad makes a good point about texting, which is why we text so often. However, it still doesn't replace face-to-face communication because the message can get lost and misinterpreted. It has happened to all of us.

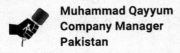

Muhammad Qayyum
Company Manager
Pakistan

Texting has, in many ways, made communication easier by helping people avoid long, unpleasant phone conversations. Text messaging is far closer to speech than formal writing, and is, in a way, a new form of communication between two or more groups. Sometimes text messages mimic the way we speak more than the way we write.

Technology can affect life both positively and negatively. New technology always changes our life very much and takes it to a new level. It is like the new way of thinking or doing the normal things differently, better and much faster with less hassle and at a much more affordable rate.

And while there are many effects of overusing technology, I think the two most serious ones are health and privacy problems.

Text messaging cannot accurately convey tone, emotion, facial expressions, gestures, body language, eye contact, oral speech, or face-to-face conversation, which means messages will likely be misinterpreted or misunderstood. The real meaning of your message gets lost through the medium.

In our day-to-day life, we use the technology in work to complete a given task. It also helps to provide a new experience in our work. It helps to complete work and it also decreases the time and helps to complete work efficiently and effectively. However, everything has a good and bad side it's totally dependent on us with how we approach this on our own.

CHAPTER FIVE

The Bad
The Physical and
Medical Side Effects

Technology is a useful servant but dangerous master.

Christian Louis Lange

Inactivity is the New Smoking!

Not moving enough may be as hazardous to our health as smoking. A study published in *The Lancet*[32] estimates as many as 5.3 million deaths around the world were caused by physical inactivity in 2008. Researchers point out that cigarette smoking is estimated to cause about five million deaths worldwide each year. Aching muscles, back pain, eye strain, carpal tunnel syndrome, headaches and weight gain are often caused by inactivity, poor posture and excessive use of tech devises.

According to the World Health Organization (WHO), a lack of physical activity is a significant risk factor for non-communicable diseases (NCDs) such as stroke, diabetes and cancer. Less and less physical activity is occurring in many countries, especially high-income countries. Globally, 81 percent of adolescents aged eleven to seventeen years were insufficiently physically active in 2016. Adolescent girls were less active than adolescent boys, with 85 percent versus 78 percent not meeting WHO recommendations of at least sixty minutes of moderate to vigorous intensity physical activity per day.[33]

Technology Addiction

Excessive use of technology can lead to addiction and several physical and social problems. If you completed the self-assessments in Chapter One, you already know if you have a problem or not. From the research I have completed and my own experience with my children, family, co-workers, clients, teachers and others, I see that this is more prevalent than we realize.

---

[32] https://www.thelancet.com/journals/lancet/article/PIIS0140-6736(12)61031-9/fulltext. "The Lancet," n.d.
[33] https://www.who.int/publications/i/item/9789240015128. "World Health Organization," n.d.

I recently met with a high school career counsellor to arrange a Txting 2 Talking presentation for a Grade 9 group. I asked her to ensure that all the students placed their phones in a ziplock bag before attending the session. She asked again how long the session would be, and I said around ninety minutes.

"Oh, that may be a problem," she said. "We have difficulty taking a phone away for a forty-minute class, let alone ninety minutes. We have had literal tantrums in our hallway because we have had to confiscate a phone and call the parents to come to pick up their deeply distressed child."

The warning signs are clear, and as parents of children that may be addicted, the responsibility lies with us. We also need to look at our own habits because we set the example and can be just as guilty.

Excessive Use

One person may spend forty hours or more per week on the Internet because his or her work depends on it. Another person may spend twenty-five hours per week chatting with family members in another country. Is this an addiction? Is it excessive? This really depends on how the time online is (or isn't) interfering with other important areas of life such as work, school, health and in-person relationships. As a general rule of thumb, however, if a person repeatedly goes online to avoid real world responsibilities or difficulties and this avoidance creates even more problems in their life, this may suggest the presence of an addiction. The signs of Internet addiction can be broken down into four distinct categories: psychological, physical, behavioural and relational.[34]

---

[34] http://www.techaddiction.ca/internet-addiction.html. "Internet Addiction," n.d.

Psychological Signs of Internet Addiction

- Frequent feelings of guilt after spending too much time online
- Great difficulty avoiding the Internet for recreational use for more than a few days in a row
- Often losing track of time when online (e.g., suddenly noticing that several hours have passed when it seems like just a few minutes)
- Strong feelings of frustration or tension when unable to go online
- Unreasonable justifications for unhealthy levels of use ("Other people are online even more than I am!")
- Downplaying the negative effects of excessive Internet use ("At least I am not addicted to drugs or alcohol")
- Loss of interest and participation in hobbies or activities that were once enjoyed
- Feeling calm, content or happy only when online
- Preoccupation with going online when engaged in other activities (e.g., school, work, or when out with friends)
- Often experiencing negative moods (depression or anxiety) when not on the Internet

Physical Signs of Internet Addiction

- Carpal tunnel syndrome
- Significant weight gain or loss due to poor eating habits and lack of physical activity
- Headaches, neck aches, back problems
- Tired, dry and/or red eyes
- Irregular, unhealthy eating habits

Param Singh
Clinical Director, Registered Physiotherapist, Owner/
Operator of Impact Health
Canada

On any given day, 30 percent of my patients suffer from postural pain. Most of these cases are related to device addiction whether that's video games, cell phones, browsing Facebook, even driving and holding a cell phone in one hand (which is illegal here—they don't report that!). Patients tell me that they play video games on their cell phones, and screen time is around three to four hours a day. They're only sleeping six hours at night because they are scrolling through Facebook on their cell phone. Scrolling at night in bed is worse than at a desk or on a laptop. More and more screen time is going to the cell phone, which is so bad for the posture. Many people don't stretch because they are not educated about it and don't know until they are in pain and must come see me.

Many of my young female patients are diagnosed with scoliosis (sideways curvature of the spine) because of excessive screen time. We X-rayed seventy girls between the ages of nine and eighteen years old last year looking for scoliosis. We found that most patients were diagnosed with non-structural scoliosis (posture related) because screen time on a device or sitting incorrectly in class or when watching TV. The fix is simple, but schools don't offer the right physical education. A simple "Keep your shoulders back and down" is all they are teaching them. Physio training is needed in the schools and for the parents because the posture and technology they are using is affecting a part of the body where there are long-term outcomes.

Why girls? They are more prone to have posture-related problems because their overall biological development is different than boys'. Typically, their bodies are not that strong compared to boys' bodies (depending on activities), they have different bone density, and there are more hormonal fluctuations in girls that impact the spine and make it more lax.

I have yet to have children of my own, so I spend my time with my two nephews aged three and a half and seven years old. The older one loves his video games and leads what I think is a sedentary lifestyle. He watches TV or Netflix, spends time on his iPad or the desktop and is essentially attached to a device most of the time. The younger one is watching him, following him and copying him. The focus needs to be on the older one, however, if my sister pulls the older one from the TV, he'll go to the desktop. If he's not on the desktop, he'll go to the iPad. His choice is always to be on a device. I've suggested that there be a time set for playtime and device time and my sister is following the advice, but when she's busy, they are back on their devices. They know that the best time to ask Mum if they can use a device is when she is busy!

In general, I need texting and messaging for my business. On the other hand, I don't want to text my parents, I want to see them. If I need to catch up with a friend, I'd rather meet in person. A text is a great way to communicate, but it's not a replacement. Human interaction is needed now more than ever. Parents are not spending enough time with their kids; they're relying on technology to communicate, and this is where they lose the human touch. Right now, the only way I can communicate with my mum is via FaceTime, but there is so much more power in seeing her in person, the kiss, the hug. If we don't use this human-to-human interaction, we will lose it.

The future impact on our youth relates to how a person learns; everyone learns differently. If you are the type of person that can learn via technology, you'll survive well and have a lot of tools at your disposal. But what if your learning style is better matched with human-to-human interaction? You will struggle.

With more people working from home, the limited in-person, face-to-face interaction takes away the "human being" part of us. Technology doesn't give us real social skills or emotional skills—a way to connect—and if we lose these skills within our own families, we cannot use them with our neighbours or society in general. If we cannot connect on a social level, would we have more crime?

In the Indian culture, we touch our elders' feet as a sign of respect, there's no swearing and we let our elders sit first. Today, kids don't listen to their parents, moral values are fading, the manners and respect are not there, and many parents simply say, "What can I do?"

We need technology as much as we need money, but it does not replace everything.

As a physiotherapist, Param sees the physical impact that is happening to our bodies due to device addiction. We often talk about the mental health impact, however, he sees both. How often have you suffered from a stiff neck or back problem related to spending too much time at your computer or on your phone? Kids and parents are consistently sitting with their heads down and playing a game or scrolling on their devices. This is bound to present a physical problem because every time your head is down you are not looking up at the person next to you.

Behavioural Signs of Internet Addiction

- Occasional "marathon" Internet sessions lasting all day or night
- Frequently eating meals in front of the computer or skipping them completely
- Regularly using the Internet until very late at night despite having to get up early the next morning

- Multiple attempts to reduce Internet use with little or no success
- Going online at virtually every opportunity
- Spending more and more time online and less time interacting with others offline
- Often going online while neglecting other important responsibilities (e.g., school, work, family, household tasks)
- Displaying anger or resentment towards those who question how much time is spent online
- If a student, decreased time spent studying and poorer academic performance

Relational Signs of Internet Addiction

- Decreased interest in sex
- Relationship problems and frequent arguments stemming from one partner spending too much time online
- Blaming one's spouse or partner for the amount of time spent on the Internet ("If you paid more attention to me, I wouldn't be online so much")
- Losing real world friends, gaining online-only friends
- Comments by others expressing concern about one's Internet use
- Decreased time spent with family and friends
- Deceiving others about the amount of time spent on the Internet

Cyberbullying

Kids call it hating, drama, gossip or trolling. Whatever name it goes by, cyberbullying is serious. It can be emotionally damaging and even lead to tragic consequences. Cyberbullying is when a child or teen is bullied by others who use computers, cell phones or other devices. It is intended to embarrass, humiliate, torment, threaten or harass the victim. It can start as early as age eight or nine, but the majority of cyberbullying takes place in the teenage years.

Understand the bystander's role in cyberbullying

While it can take just one teen to start the humiliation or harassment of another, bystanders play an essential role in perpetuating the bullying and giving it power and momentum.

 It's very easy to make a nasty comment when you don't have to say it to a person's face. You can hide behind your phone and there's really no consequences, which is why this form of bullying is so rampant. Another side, however, is sometimes a nasty comment posted online is shamed by the community it's posted in and this can discredit or disgrace the commenter. But then it is a vicious cycle back and forth. When does it end?

What is a bystander?

A passive bystander sees cyberbullying taking place and does nothing. They may receive a copy of a cyberbullying message or photo. They may see an attack taking place on a social network or they might get asked to vote in an online poll intended to hurt someone. While they don't actively participate, they do nothing to stop it. Their silence gives the bully permission to continue.

An active bystander is someone who joins the bullying. Their participation may be no more than forwarding a photo or message to their friends, which gives the bullies a wider audience and spreads the humiliation. Or it may be encouraging them by "liking" things posted on social networks, adding comments that spur them on or even joining in active bullying once it has begun.

Either way, it's important to talk with your child about their role in cyberbullying and how they may be contributing to another child's harm.

Help your child stand up to cyberbullying

Everyone—including our children—must work together to put an end to cyberbullying. We can encourage our kids to take a stand by using the steps below:

- Let them know how bystanders—both passive and active—are part of the problem and help the bully gain more power and hurt the victim.
- Encourage empathy. Help your child put themselves in someone else's position to imagine how they would feel. How would they feel if this were being said or done to their sibling, cousin or other friends?
- Encourage them to never forward humiliating messages, texts or photos to their friends, or respond or make comments on cyberbullying posts.
- Teach your child to never say something online they wouldn't feel comfortable saying to someone's face.
- Talk to them about how they could tell their friends they won't take part in any cyberbullying.
- If they see cyberbullying on a site like Facebook, show them how they can report it as abusive. Facebook has introduced a Cyberbullying Prevention Hub where users can report that a friend is being bullied (or that they've been bullied themselves). Most social networking sites have reporting features built in to flag abusive content.

- Let them know that if they know someone is being cyberbullied, they should report it to you, a teacher or to another adult they trust.
- They can fill out an anonymous letter and drop it off with a teacher or school office.
- If they know the victim personally, they can help the victim by acknowledging what they're going through and help them to report it to an adult and find support.
- If they are friends with the person doing the cyberbullying, they can send a message saying they're uncomfortable with what they're seeing and ask them to stop.
- Share any examples you know of where someone taking a stand on someone else's behalf had a positive outcome.
- Empower your child/teen to deal with the situation by providing them with information such as the NeedHelpNow.ca website where they can find information on how to deal with others or how to have pictures/videos removed from the Internet.[35]

The hardest thing for your child to do may be to take an active stand, but if you can help them feel safe enough to do so, it can have a lot of impact. Using neutral language, they can comment on a bullying post or photo by writing something like: "I'm going to hide this or unfollow this because I think it's hurtful. I encourage others to do the same." Or, in the case of persistent bullying, they could write: "I'm going to block this person because I think what they're doing is hurtful. I hope other people will do the same." Many children know cyberbullying is wrong and will join in once one person has shown the courage to step forward.

---

[35] https://www.canada.ca/en/public-safety-canada/campaigns/cyberbullying.html. "Cyberbullying," n.d

Child Exploitation

An unfortunate reality of life in the Internet world is that it has become a place where predators lurk. It is important for parents to understand the risks of allowing their kids online and what steps to take to prevent them from being taken advantage of.

A predator who targets children will typically try to attain explicit photos of children (or to share photos of their own), will want to meet the child in person to involve them in sexual activity or try to engage them in sexual conversations or online role play. The predator will lie to children about their age, but they will also register as younger people when signing up for an online account on social media sites like Instagram and Snapchat. It is important to discuss online safety. The key is to have honest discussions around the following:

- What could happen if they become a victim? A child should feel comfortable coming to a parent without fear of retribution if they end up in a dangerous situation
- Whom to talk to and whom to avoid
- Sharing personal information
- The stages of grooming. How predators get kids to share information through compliments, liking or commenting on their posts, and stating that they have the same interests. As well, they may ask questions about the parents and if they monitor their online activity[36]

Open communication with your children will reduce the likelihood of them becoming a victim.

---

[36] https://www.understood.org/en/articles/9-ways-to-protect-your-child-from-online-predators. "Online Predators," n.d.

Mandy Brown
Police Officer
Canada

Because of my line of work, I am hyperaware of the risks and dangers out there with respect to predators and bullying. This hypervigilance makes us (my husband is also a police officer) extremely cautious with respect to unsupervised use of technology. For this reason, my stepdaughter is not allowed to have a phone. It's not that we don't trust her but because we don't trust others; she is also the only one in her class without one, which she says she is fine with.

We have had open discussions regarding the dangers and what some people may try to do (without making her paranoid). We do not sugar-coat the truth or use fluffy words; we go straight to the point so that no confusion can occur regarding what we are discussing. We also use proper anatomical words and don't use nicknames. We discuss things that a person, be it stranger or not, may say to try and create that trust so that she will send photos.

The more aware children are, the more likely they are to tell their parents or someone they trust if something happens. They can also accurately describe their understanding of what the person was trying to illicit.

My advice to parents is to be completely open and honest with your children when discussing Internet safety. You are not trying to scare them, but you are making sure they are aware there are people out there who will try to take advantage of kids; they need to be conscious of it. Using age-appropriate wording, discuss the possible scenarios and what predators may do to make children trust them online. Make sure that they know to NEVER send pictures or share any personal information with people, and that if anyone asks for photos or says anything that makes them uncomfortable they should tell their parents (with the caveat that they are NOT in trouble).

Always know your kids' passwords and tell them you will be checking the messaging, etc., just to ensure their safety (not because they can't be trusted). Sometimes a child may think something is okay to say or send, but it doesn't mean that it is, so this is another reason for monitoring.

Keep the tech out of the bedrooms and not behind closed doors as much as possible; no tech after bedtime (a lot of cyberbullying sees kids up all hours of the night on their technology). Limit screen time (you can adjust the settings). Create a setting where they cannot purchase an app without your approval; you will get the notification and make the decision whether to allow it or not (works for free apps).

Research Internet safety. A great site is the Canadian Centre for Child Protection. The more you know, the better. The RCMP website and the Bullying Canada website both have good information to help you discuss this with your children.

Encourage your kids to limit their screen time, to participate in social activities, to have good conversations at mealtimes. This will help them feel comfortable sharing if something "bad" were ever to happen to them online.

As police officers, Mandy and her husband are fully aware of the dangers of children being unsupervised when using technology. She makes some great points about how to tackle this and how to have those open and honest conversations now before something happens. The website in the footnote has some good resources.[37]

---

[37] https://www.rcmp-grc.gc.ca/en/bullying. "Cyberbullying," n.d.

Brain Function

Depending on which study you come across, there seems to be more evidence supporting a correlation between adverse brain function, increased screen time and Internet addiction. One study released in 2013 looked at gray matter atrophy (shrinkage or loss of tissue volume) in gray matter areas (where "processing" occurs) in Internet/gaming addiction. Areas affected included the important frontal lobe, which governs executive functions such as planning, prioritizing, organizing and impulse control ("getting stuff done").[38] The study showed that "Internet addiction disorder subjects may have abnormal frontal lobe function due to partial neuronal loss. To a certain extent, the cell membrane function of neurons may be damaged." If you search for Internet Gaming Disorder (IGD) (defined as "a persistent and recurrent involvement with video games, often leading to significant impairments of daily, work and/or educational activities"), you will find more recent studies that suggest that IGD is often accompanied by lack of sleep, depression, hostility and social anxiety.

Radio Frequency and Cell Phones

The debate about whether cell phones cause cancer is ongoing, and there are studies that support the cancer scare or debunk it. Either way, it is fair to assume that the studies are out there and more are coming as we continue on our path to include more and more technology in our lives. The key culprit is the radio frequency that cell phones emit.

When turned on, cell phones and other wireless devices continually emit radiofrequency (RF) radiation even if they are not being actively used because they are always communicating with cell

---

[38] https://www.ncbi.nlm.nih.gov/pmc/articles/PMC4146181/.
"National Institutes of Health," n.d.

towers. The dose intensity tails off with increasing distance from the body and reaches a maximum when the devices are used next to the head during phone calls or in front of the body when using a device. In a ten-year US Food and Drug Administration study, they dosed rats and mice of both sexes with RF radiation. The animals were exposed nine hours a day for two years (about the average life span for a rat), and the exposures were cranked up steadily as the animals grew, so the absorbed doses per unit of body weight remained constant over time. In 2016, results from the study showed evidence that RF energy may be linked to cancer in those lab rodents. The strongest finding connected RF with heart schwannomas (a tumour that grows in the sheaths of nerves in your peripheral nervous system or the parts of your nervous system that aren't in your brain or spinal cord) in male rats, but the researchers also reported elevated rates of lymphoma as well as cancers affecting the prostate, skin, lung, liver and brain in the exposed animals.[39]

What Do Expert Organizations Say?

In 2011, the International Agency for Research on Cancer (IARC), a component of the WHO, appointed an expert working group to review all available evidence on the use of cell phones. The working group classified cell phone use as "possibly carcinogenic to humans" based on limited evidence from human studies, limited evidence from studies of RF energy and cancer in rodents, and inconsistent evidence from mechanistic studies.

The American Cancer Society (ACS) states that the IARC classification means that there could be some cancer risk associated with RF energy, but the evidence is not strong enough to be

---

[39] https://www.fda.gov/radiation-emitting-products/cell-phones/
scientific-evidence-cell-phone-safety. "US Food & Drug Administration," n.d.

considered causal and needs to be investigated further. Individuals who are concerned about RF energy exposure can limit their exposure by using an ear piece and limiting cell phone use, particularly among children.[40]

Dr. Devra Davis founded the non-profit Environmental Health Trust in 2007 in Teton County, Wyoming, to provide basic research and education about environmental health hazards and promote constructive policies locally, nationally and internationally. Their vision is: "A thriving world where technology is both state of the art and safe for all." Their mission is: "To safeguard human health and the environment by empowering people with state-of-the-art information." Dr. Davis' presentation to the University of Melbourne on cell phone radiation is a scary eye-opener. You can view this on YouTube, and the Environmental Health Trust has some amazing fact sheets that everyone should read. The "What Parents Need to Know About Safe Technology" fact sheet[41] is a good place to start. It highlights the following:

What Does the Science Say about Wireless and Children?

- Children have thinner skulls. Research shows that children's developing brains, eyes and bone marrow absorb this radiation three to ten times more than adults.
- A 2018 study found memory damage in teenagers who used cell phones near the head for just one year.[42] Research links wireless to hyperactivity, behaviour problems and damaged sperm.

---

[40]   https://www.cancer.gov/about-cancer/causes-prevention/risk/ radiation/cell-phones-fact-sheet. "National Cancer Institute," n.d.

[41]   https://ehtrust.org/resources-to-share/printable-resources/. "Environmental Health Trust," n.d.

[42]   https://www.ncbi.nlm.nih.gov/pmc/articles/PMC6108834/. "National Library of Medicine," n.d.

Read the Fine Print

Actual information included in user manuals:

- "When placing Apple Watch near your face, keep at least 10mm of separation."
- "Keep safe distance from pregnant women's stomachs or from lower stomach of teenagers." (Samsung 3G laptop manual)

American Academy of Pediatrics Safety Tips for Families

- Use cell phones in speaker mode or with the use of hands-free kits.
- Avoid carrying your phone against the body like in a pocket, sock or bra. Cell phone manufacturers can't guarantee that the amount of radiation you're absorbing will be at a safe level.
- If you plan to watch a movie on your device, download it first then switch to airplane mode while you watch to avoid unnecessary radiation exposure.
- Keep an eye on your signal strength (i.e., how many bars you have). The weaker your cell signal, the harder your phone must work and the more radiation it emits.
- Avoid making calls in cars, elevators, trains and buses. The cell phone works harder to get a signal through metal, so the power level increases.
- Remember that cell phones are not toys or teething items.
- Make only short or essential calls on cell phones.

New Jersey Education Association Review 11/2016

Minimize health risks from electronic devices by:

- Keeping devices away from the body and bedroom

- Putting devices on desks, not laps
- Hardwiring all devices that connect to the Internet
- Hardwiring all fixed devices such as printers, projectors and boards
- Use hardwired phones instead of cell or cordless phones.

Ian Malcolm, *Jurassic Park*

In the 1993 film *Jurassic Park*, mathematician Ian Malcolm, who was played by Jeff Goldblum, summed up the dangers of the digital world when he said, "Your scientists were so preoccupied with whether or not they could that they didn't stop to think if they should."

When issues arise and studies are reporting disturbing statistics from device use, tech companies need to see the bigger picture and invest time and money to address, or at least support, initiatives that are trying to alleviate ever growing tech addictions. With new technologies like artificial intelligence (AI) becoming more and more mainstream, another quote by Ian Malcolm comes to mind: "I'll tell you the problem with the scientific power that you're using here. It didn't require any discipline to attain it."

Privacy

Have you ever been online searching for that tropical vacation in Mexico and an ad pops up in Facebook the next day for 40 percent off Mexican vacations? At first, I thought the universe was speaking to me and that I was meant to spend my savings on a luxury resort in Cancun. Little did I know that Google and

Facebook closely monitor the websites a person visits so they can promote ads that match the person's interests.

It seems that nothing is private anymore, and everyone seems to know something about everything we do even if the information is not that important. Sadly, we are the ones perpetuating it. Do you share specifics about your doctor visits, vacations, kids on social media? Be aware that you are being watched, and a gold mine of personal information is being returned to corporations and governments that shows what you buy, where you travel and how healthy you are.

 ## Our Personal Data: Thomas P Keenan, Technocreep[43]

Who is mining Twitter for our thoughts and emotions? It turns out that our social networks are catnip for marketers seeking to learn all about us. Think about all the things you post on social media, from your age to your sexual orientation, religious beliefs and perhaps even that you were just laid off from your job. Now think about some of the most powerful computer and predictive analytics tools being used to analyze your every tweet. Thomas Keenan, author of Technocreep, advises keeping your medical records and DNA to yourself, use two-step verification and clear the GPS records in a rental car.

---

[43] https://www.cbc.ca/radio/thecurrent/satire-online-creeping-and-the-fascinating-facts-about-twins-1.2906987/technocreep-author-exposes-just-how-much-creeping-goes-on-online-1.2906990. "'Technocreep' Author Exposes Just How Much Creeping Goes on Online," n.d.

Identity Theft

Chances are you or someone you know has had their identity stolen. The impact is great not only on your money and time but the emotional toll it takes to get your identity back. At the end of the day, it is a crime and you could be the next victim. In 2017, there were 16.7 million victims of identity fraud, a record high that followed a previous record the year before. Criminals are using complex identity fraud schemes and you could be next. The amount stolen hit $16.8 billion in 2017, and it's getting worse.[44]

The Cybercriminal

Brett Johnson was a cybercriminal. He was caught using fake cashiers' cheques, and the secret service brought him in as an informant. That didn't stop him, and he continued to steal using computers at FedEx Kinko's locations to file fake tax returns and direct the money to prepaid credit cards. He eventually plead guilty in 2007 on charges of fraud, received six months in prison and had to pay back his victims over $300,000. Today Brett is doing the job he used to tell his victims he was doing when he was scamming them: fraud consulting.[45]

The Impact of Identity theft

Victims of identity theft suffer much the same way a survivor of a robbery or any other trauma would. According to Diane Turner, a licensed clinical social worker and certified life coach, victims often experience emotional effects and exhibit signs of grief similar to depression and heightened anxiety. They report loss of confidence in areas where they typically had confidence, sleeplessness, emotional

---

[44]   https://www.iii.org/fact-statistic/facts-statistics-identity-theft-and-cybercrime. "Identity Theft and Cybercrime," n.d.

[45]   https://money.cnn.com/2017/11/28/pf/cybercrime-identity-thief/index.html. "Meet the Man Who Used to Steal Your Identity," n.d.

volatility, difficulty eating, self-medicating with alcohol or food, and loss of motivation. Equifax, a consumer credit reporting agency, interviewed experts and victims who deal with these issues daily and produced a white paper that examines the symptoms that identity theft victims may experience and why. They also outline the steps victims can take to help themselves and advice on how to best minimize the likelihood of identity theft in the first place. If you are a victim of identity theft, some steps include:

- Check your credit report with all three credit reporting agencies.
- Block or close fraudulent accounts.
- Remember to keep checking your credit report regularly; it can take months for a new account to show up on your report.
- Place a fraud alert by contacting any one of the three credit reporting agencies.
- File a police report. Report the crime to the Federal Trade Commission.
- Don't panic and think worst-case scenarios. Stay in the present and make a plan.
- Take care of yourself and surround yourself with supportive people.
- Keep a detailed journal of every call you make, every letter you receive.
- Contact a victims' assistance group. They can lead you through the process of fixing the issue.
- Consider getting professional help. Pay attention to your mental state and seek out counsel if you need it.
- Come to terms with the crime. Accept the challenge that the crime has presented, but recognize your power and ability to move forward.[46]

---

[46]   https://assets.equifax.com/legacy/assets/PSOL/15-9814_psol_emotionalToll_wp.pdf. "A Lasting Impact: The Emotional Toll of Identity Theft," n.d.

Jeff Provost
Parent, IT Security Analyst for IBM, Former Military
Canada

I have two girls (four and seven) and a boy (twelve). They all have their own iPad/iPhone. There's a PC available for the whole family.

I think our reality with this new generation is something that we must start getting used to. Of course, my childhood was so different, but life in general was also very different. Parents didn't care as much where we were, and all they asked was for us to make sure that we were back for dinner or in time for bed. Today's parents tend to cover them, and we don't let them be kids the same way our parents did. I think this is a normal progression in our society.

The "always connected lifestyle" is part of our life now, but education will remain the key factor as to what this lifestyle will look like in the future. In terms of the dangers of tech addiction, I don't think there's a secret sauce to it. Trying to keep a balance between tech and no tech is the key. Playing soccer outside with friends will help them understand that they can be doing something else.

The gap between people that understand this technology and the ones who don't will be much smaller, so parents and schools will be able to educate our kids more effectively on how to keep a well-balanced lifestyle. It may take a few generations before we can close that gap, but I think we must be patient.

I currently work in IT security for a big international company, and I can tell you that the danger online is everywhere. But I am always asking myself if I'm going to stop living and stop enjoying technology because the danger is everywhere. No! Am I going to stop my children from enjoying it? No! It would be easy to become paranoid about everything around you when you are constantly reading about companies being breached or even people getting their phone hacked through text messaging (which is something that happened recently to the owner of Amazon, Jeff Bezos). Remember, almost everything is on the Internet so if there's something you are not willing to share with the world, don't put it on the Internet even if it says it will remain private; it could come back to haunt you.

Children need to be taught about cybersecurity at a young age. We keep reminding them of the dangers of talking to strangers or watching what they put in their mouths because of bacteria and getting sick. Cybersecurity is a new danger, and we need to talk about it before it's too late. Hackers use a technique called social engineering; this has been made very popular by one of the most wanted hackers in the United States, Kevin Mitnick. This technique targets the human psychological flaw that tricks kids into giving something of value like login and password information.

The Apple environment has a tool to control our kids' play time on the whole platform or you can customize it one app at a time. Microsoft also has a tool that helps you control access to your kids play time on a PC or Xbox. Another device, made by Disney, helps limit their time on the Internet and makes sure they are not going on an unwanted website. Ultimately, I still think that we need to remain flexible, and parents need to adapt themselves to each kid. I would be lying if I said my three kids are treated the same. Behaviour, age, etc. are all factors that affect their access, which is evaluated on an almost daily basis. A family is like managing a small organization, and not every employee is the same.

Parents must recognize the symptoms of addiction. It might be hard for a four-year-old to understand the concept, but this is where parents have to be alert. It will be natural to them eventually if we coach them at an early age about how to manage this. Constantly educating our kids on what is out there without scaring them is important. They need to understand how a good and healthy mental and physical balance is important.

We must teach them that Facebook or Instagram isn't the reality. It's not because we see someone going on vacation that we must assume they are always having a good time. They also have their lows as well. When you have a friend list of one thousand people, this is unrealistic because they are not all real friends, and the chances of seeing someone doing a fun activity is quite high; not everyone is having fun. If our kids start building on this, they will be quite disappointed in the future.

Human interaction remains important in our society. Our kids need to know this and relate to a real "live" person to feel they are loved and important to us and that no matter what happens we are there for them.

Education, education, and again education.

I'm not perfect, but I think I am doing pretty well now. I still love technology, and I am not going to hide behind a mask. I have more toys than I need, but most of them support our complex life. I like to think that I am setting a good example and try to keep a good balance between the two. My current career is based in technology, so it is hard for me to step away all the time. When my kids are around me, I try to put my phone down, close the lid of my laptop or even turn down the volume of the TV just to hear, talk or laugh with them.

Gaming has been an addiction I've experienced in the past. Social workers understand the addiction of drugs and alcohol, but gaming is fairly new, and they don't seem to have the right tools to help those who need it (according to my experience). I eventually understood what I needed to do to overcome this addiction. Today, I barely play any type of game, and I find a way to occupy my mind and do something else. Now that I understand the issue, I pass it on to my family. My wife is also good with this, and she likes to organize a lot of activities outside the house and away from technology.

Apple came up with a new setting in iOS called "Screen Time." It lets me track my activities, set limit times and much more. It's a good way for a self-conscious person like me to analyse where I'm spending most of my time. If I have been spending too much time on Facebook, I should find a way to decrease it or put a limit per day. Android must have a similar app.

I don't think my parents' generation completely understood my generation, and I don't think my generation completely understands this new generation. Technology is constantly moving forward, but we like to think about the past, like when we were kids. I don't think there's anything wrong with the past and how we used to live, but technology was at a different level. Now, we have to turn the page and keep shaping this new narrative to ensure the next few generations understand what is at stake.

Technology and connected lives have helped develop our nation at an incredible pace and way faster than anyone can believe. We just must understand its behaviour, study it and then start taming it as a nation. We can't be afraid of its capability, but we must always keep security in mind.

When I speak with someone in IT security, I always come away more informed but a little scared as to what's happening out there. I hear of hacking and data breaches, phishing and child luring on a regular basis. Jeff is hyperaware, he knows the risks, he can recognize his and his kids' potential for addiction and its consequences. He is also a realist, so he understands that technology is a part of our lives that must be managed.

 ## Teaching Cybersecurity to Children Starts at Home [47]

Teaching cybersecurity to your children starts with a chat about being responsible and smart. Kerry Matre of Hewlett Packard Enterprises also recommends that you encourage children to verify with you if something doesn't seem right and to realize that their identity is sacred.

Due to online predators, children need to be wary about what personal information they reveal online, especially personal data like their name, age and location. Even an online photo of your child could be a hazard if he or she is wearing a T-shirt with the logo of their school; that school could be easily tracked down by a predator.

Make sure your kids know that any information or images they post on the Internet have the potential to stay on the Internet forever, even after they've been deleted. That includes Twitter tweets, Facebook posts and Snapchat images captured by a screenshot.

Parents who are thinking about giving their children smartphones should first gauge the child's maturity level and cyber knowledge. Take the time to turn the gift of a

---

[47]   https://apuedge.com/cybersecurity-best-practices-for-teaching-it-to-your-kids/. "American Public University," n.d.

smartphone into a cyber education experience. Teach that child how to create a strong password, how to refuse requests for inappropriate images and how to block unwanted, unknown people.

Also, use the parental controls on the smartphone can prevent a child from downloading a potentially dangerous app without your knowledge.

The "bad" effects are having an impact on our physical and mental health, and especially on our children. And we're not done. I have a couple more to outline before we move on to the "ugly" effects.

Losing the Ability to Communicate

The statistics in Chapter Three ("How Do We Communicate Today?") are alarming. Texting, e-mail, social media and gaming have become more prevalent over the years. In many cases, technology has taken the place of us "speaking," and so we have, as a generation, become increasingly uncomfortable with how to communicate well. I have facilitated many workshops on communication and business networking where participants state that they didn't know how to start a conversation with someone. They not only didn't know what to say, I had to give them examples and use role plays. They also felt that they were imposing on or bothering the other person by wanting to speak with them. That's what you get when 90 percent of your day is spent communicating via text, e-mail or social media: you lose the art of conversation, and the next generation, having spent a good portion of their young lives on their devices, are really struggling.

Connecting: Quantity over Quality?

Although being connected to everyone and everything has its advantages, we must ask, "Are we becoming more electronically networked but more personally isolated?" Are our Facebook friends really our true friends whom we can call in the middle of the night in case of an emergency? Of course not. The more time we spend online, the less time we have for actual real-life social interactions, and when we do get that precious human-to-human time it seems many of us, especially our youth, have lost the ability to communicate and form relationships. This can lead to low confidence, poor self-esteem and increased isolation. Friendship is about being authentic and genuine. It's about sharing values, establishing trust and engaging in meaningful conversations. Is having more friends a remedy for loneliness or is spending more time with those you are closest to better? Do we need one thousand friends on Facebook or could we be trying to make a positive connection with an existing friend that we really relate to? Quality friendships over quantity are much more satisfying, and in the long run they outweigh thousands of online friendships.

This final survey outlines how isolated we have become.

Social Media Use and Perceived Social Isolation Among Young Adults in the U.S[48]

Brian Primack MD, PhD and a group of colleagues surveyed 1,787 US adults aged nineteen to thirty-two and asked them about their usage of eleven social media platforms outside of work. The survey also gauged social isolation by asking participants questions such as how often they felt left out. The people who reported spending the most time on social media (more than two hours a

---

[48]   https://pubmed.ncbi.nlm.nih.gov/28279545/. "National Library of Medicine," n.d.

day) had twice the odds of perceived social isolation than those who said they spent a half hour per day or less on those sites. And people who visited social media platforms most frequently (fifty-eight visits per week or more) had more than three times the odds of perceived social isolation than those who visited fewer than nine times per week.

The study also suggests that interacting and communicating with others online versus just observing other people's lives has an impact on how isolated people feel. It states, "Your peers' lives may elicit feelings of envy and the distorted belief that others lead happier and more successful lives, which may increase perceived social isolation."

So there you have it, the "bad." That was a lot to take in. Now we move on to the "ugly" effects. And you thought the bad was bad!

CHAPTER SIX

The Ugly
Texting, Driving & Distraction: Under the Influence of Cell Phones

The worst thing about the miracle of modern communications is the Pavlovian pressure it places upon everyone to communicate whenever a bell rings.

Russell Baker

Have you ever stopped at a red light only to notice that the driver beside you is on their cell phone texting? Did you notice the teen strolling across the crosswalk, headphones on and texting away oblivious to the world around her? These situations happen regularly and are resulting in some tragic accidents.

Imagine picking up a Rubik's Cube and starting to solve it while you're driving. Risky? Yes. Your concentration is on the Cube, even if it's only for a few seconds. In the same way, driving while texting increases your chance of crashing by twenty-three times. Talking or listening to a cell phone conversation increases this risk by 1.3 times. The average time to answer a text is 4.6 seconds, so if you are driving at fifty-five miles per hour, this is equivalent to driving the length of a football field blind. According to the National Safety Council, cell phone use while driving leads to 1.6 million crashes annually.[49] The facts are startling:

- About 26 percent of all car crashes involve phone use, including hands-free phone use. (National Safety Council)
- Estimates indicate drivers using phones look at, but fail to see, up to 50 percent of the information in their driving environment. (National Safety Council, 2012)
- Drivers conversing on mobile devices, either hands-free or handheld, are up to four times as likely to be involved in a crash. (AAA Foundation for Traffic Safety, 2017)
- 80 percent of collisions and 65 percent of near crashes have some form of driver inattention as contributing factors. (National Highway Traffic Safety Administration, 2010)
- Driver distraction is a factor in about four million motor vehicle crashes in North America each year. (RCMP, 2014)

---

[49]   https://www.nsc.org/getmedia/2ea8fe8b-d7b7-4194-8ea5-306d30a73972/cognitive-distraction-white-paper.pdf. "Cognitive Distraction," n.d.

- 10 percent of fatal crashes, 18 percent of injury crashes, and 16 percent of all police-reported motor vehicle crashes were distraction-affected. (National Highway Safety Administration, 2015)
- Distraction was a factor in nearly six out of ten moderate to severe teen crashes. (AAA Foundation for Traffic Safety, 2015)
- Almost half of all people killed in teen (fifteen to nineteen years old) distraction-affected crashes were teens themselves. (National Highway Traffic Safety Administration, 2013)

Scary stuff! And there's more.

Distracted Driving; "I don't know what happened; I was just on my phone."

The National Safety Council created the Annual Estimate of Cell Phone Crashes because data about cell phone use as a factor in motor vehicle crashes is currently under-reported. When the police attempt to collect this data, they rely almost entirely on driver self-reports or witness reports of cell phone use at the time of the crash, which results in significant under-reporting.

Below, I refer to cities, provinces, states, countries and even corporations that have taken a serious stance on distracted driving to help lower these statistics, but it seems drivers are still not getting the message. Apparently, it is more important to take that important call or text that asks them to "Pick up milk AND bread" on their way home.

Strong Laws in Utah!

On July 1, 2009, the state of Utah in the US took a strong stand. The new law forbids texting while driving, and the punishment for violating the law is the harshest in the country: up to fifteen years in prison. The state government feels that all drivers are now educated enough about the dangers of texting while driving to classify any such behaviour as reckless or negligent driving.

"It's a willful act," said Lyle Hillyard, a Republican state senator and a big supporter of the new measure. "If you choose to drink and drive or if you choose to text and drive, you're assuming the same risk."

The severity of the punishment is believed to have been so well-supported because of an accident that occurred three years before that resulted in the deaths of two scientists, and there are many other tragic accidents reported and attributed to texting while driving. In fact, more US states now have penalties in place with fines increasing for primary and secondary offences.

Canada Gets it Right

All ten provinces have some form of distracted driving legislation in place, with the highest fine in the country going up to $888 in British Columbia on the second offence. Manitoba and Prince Edward Island are tied for first in deducting the highest number of demerit points, up to five, for distracted driving offences.

My research indicates there is a debate as to whether a cell phone ban (restricting drivers from using handheld cell phones, texting or e-mailing or any other electronic devices such as laptops and iPads even while stopped at red lights) will actually reduce accidents. Some results showed a reduction in distracted driving accidents, but only slightly. Others showed a reduction only for a short time mostly due to a lack of continuous awareness in the community it served. And let's face it, unless the fine or punishment is high, people aren't concerned about it.

In the United States

The law of July 1, 2009, in Utah is also difficult to police and enforce, as I have discovered, although police are finding new tactics to catch the culprits. In Bethesda, Maryland, a police officer disguised himself as an unhoused man, stood near a busy intersection and radioed ahead to officers down the road about texting drivers. In two hours, police issued fifty-six tickets.

And in West Bridgewater, Massachusetts, an officer regularly tools around town on his bicycle, pedals up to drivers at stoplights and hands them $105 tickets.

Our days are often full of many to-dos, most of which are job related. Productivity is expected to be high in our fast-paced world. Co-workers and clients expect answers immediately and are stunned when they don't get them. Some corporations are looking at implementing cell phone use while driving policies, but most aren't. Productivity concerns are often cited as one of the top obstacles to implementing a total ban according to the National Safety Council. For instance, if your sales force typically spends the bulk of the workday on the phone talking to potential customers while driving between appointments, a cell phone ban could negatively impact the business. And yet, in surveys within companies, there does not appear to be a significant negative impact on productivity cited.

In 2009, the National Safety Council surveyed 469 members that had implemented total cell phone bans.[50] Only 1 percent reported that productivity decreased. In the 2010 National Safety Council survey of Fortune 500 companies, of the ones that had cell phone

---

[50] https://www.nsc.org/getmedia/384375ad-b156-426e-b414-bc6481511d00/nsc-corpliability-wp.pdf.aspx. "Employer Liability and the Case for Comprehensive Cell Phone Policies," n.d.

bans in place, only 7 percent said productivity decreased while 19 percent thought productivity had actually increased.

As we move forward, it's clear that we must take responsibility when we are driving. And it begins at home. We need to put our phones down once we get behind the wheel and ask our loved ones to do the same. Until laws adapt or we find new ways to combat this there are organizations that are leading the way in educating the public about the dangers of distracted driving. I have included many in this chapter, but ultimately the responsibility lies with us. A good source for young adults is Young Drivers of Canada. I'll leave you with one story from Bernadette McCrea in March of 201551 that begs us to reconsider the next time we pick up our phone in the car.

Don't Text and Drive

On July 29, 2006, as I was crossing the street in a crosswalk in Newark, New Jersey, an SUV ran through the red light, hit me and dragged me half a block. It was around 5:00 p.m., and extremely hot. I felt the skin of my legs burning on the ground. I tried to get up, but I couldn't. My legs wouldn't move. I tried to look up, see where I was, but I was blinded by the blood in my eyes that was pouring down from my wounded head. I screamed for help, for someone to please help me get off the ground. I've never felt so much pain in all my life.

Finally, there was someone at my side who called an ambulance and stayed with me until they came. He had been in his car at the red light, saw it happen and came to my aid. He was my lifesaver. I would have bled to death had I not made it to the hospital in time. My lifesaver also saw that the driver was on her cell phone.

---

51 https://yd.com/stop-distracted-driving. "How Young Drivers of Canada Prevents Distracted Driving," n.d.

I had to have a blood transfusion and 150 staples put in my head. I suffered a brain injury, a fractured skull and a bone in my neck was crushed. I broke my collarbone, several ribs, my pelvis, my hip was dislocated and fractured, and my ankle was completely broken on both sides. I was in the hospital for a long time before being transferred to a rehab hospital. I had to wear a neck brace, hip brace and a big boot. I had to use a wheelchair and a walker.

My life completely changed that day. I can't even begin to explain the amount of pain that I suffered, how hard it was to recover and how frustrating it is that this destruction was caused by poor judgement. It was eight years ago, and though I've healed in many ways, there's parts of me that will never be the same. I take every day as it comes and deal with the pain and the grief the best I can. Life is a precious, fragile gift, and it's so unfair to rob someone of that gift because you're distracted on the phone while driving. Whatever needs to be said can't possibly be more important than another person's life—or even your own—it can wait. Please, share my story to remind people of the pain that can be caused by driving distracted. Please text responsibly.

The Good

What would we do without our many devices? Our lives depend on these additions to our existence, and advancement in technology is ongoing by the second! Change is a constant. Whether it's related to health, education, feeling more secure or simply making our lives easier, there are many reasons why we love living in this new age. Without the Internet, however, most of our devices are relatively useless.

Some questions for you

- What technology, app or device have you adopted that makes your life easier, has made you feel more secure or simply has changed how you communicate?
- How has this changed your life? Good or bad?

The Bad

OK, so it looks bad. And I only highlighted *some* examples of the "bad," there are many more that highlight the issues we're facing with tech addiction. Many people are aware of the problem, but I'm afraid that the addictions are deepening and becoming worse. Every parent, teacher, co-worker, friend and acquaintance I speak with tell me it's bad and increasing at a fast pace.

Some Questions for You

- Have you had your identity stolen? People I know who have had this happen tell me it's a nightmare. What advice would you give others to prevent this?
- Do you know of someone who exhibits all the signs of addiction to technology? What could you do to help? The self-assessments in Chapter One might be a good start.
- What do you think about the effects of radio frequencies? Does it concern you now, especially with regards to your child's excessive and constant use of their cell phone?
- Have you tried to have a conversation with a fourteen-year-old? Can they look you in the eye or is it difficult to get them away from their phone?

The Ugly

As the statistics state, texting and driving is a major problem, but texting and walking can be too! Let's face it, nothing is so important that we need to be texting while operating a vehicle, yet people do this every day.

Some Questions for You

Which statistics surprised you? Was it the average time to answer a text (4.6 seconds)? If you are driving at fifty-five miles per hour, this is equivalent to driving the length of a football field blind.

Have you texted while driving? When was the last time?

Did this information convince you to put your phone down? Can you convince others?

As with anything in life, there is always the good, the bad and the ugly. Typical advice is to focus on the good, minimize the bad and do your best to eliminate the ugly. Before diving into the next chapter, here are some more questions to ponder.

- With the world moving at a fast pace, technology moving faster and with virtual communication coming at us from everywhere, how can we manage it all?
- Can we turn it all off? Do we want to?
- When was the last time you had a meaningful conversation, one on one and in person with another human being?
- Where do we draw the line on our dependency to our devices, the Internet, social media? Do we have a line?
- What could you give up?

CHAPTER SEVEN

Disconnect to Reconnect
and
The Art of Conversation

Life is what happens when your cell phone is charging.

Unknown

Disconnect to Reconnect

Do you wish your teen would have a real conversation with you?

Are you waiting for the day when you can have a meaningful talk with your partner without the phone *dinging* in the background?

Is it possible to eat a meal with the family where everyone is excited to talk about their day as opposed to burying their heads and intensely concentrating on nothing in particular on their phone?

Shouldn't be too much to ask, right?

Many parents, business owners, doctors, speakers and teens I have spoken with agree that they spend too much time glued to their phone. Parents were excited when I told them I was writing this book and have presented this topic to local schools. I believe they were secretly hoping I would give them all the answers so they could finally connect with their kids, partner and family again. What I realized after having many of these conversations is that I simply needed to say, "It starts with you!"

Bentley Jordan
Student and Young Entrepreneur
Canada

I own an Android tablet, and I spend about ten hours a week on social media, texting or surfing the Internet. My parents limit my Internet time and have not let me have a phone yet! Since I have limited time with technology, I have felt left out and bored when spending time with my friends who are all on their phones. After seeing how much time is spent on electronics, I came up with a new business idea: phone bags to keep your phones in and away from you so you are not on them all the time. I create messages for the bags like: "Put me down, read a book," "Put me to sleep zzzzzzzz," and "Don't touch me, bake some cookies." My business is called Bentley's Bags!

It is refreshing to see that Bentley recognized what was happening with his friends and their devices at such a young age. To create a business idea out of it takes it to the next level! Kudos to his parents, who believed in limiting access to technology to encourage more time for other things—they created an entrepreneur.

Unplugging

It's not easy to unplug. Our attachment to our devices is a strong one. This book has outlined all the ways we have become addicted. We also create our online personas, we chat on social media and play games with weird, fake usernames, so we are also detaching from our real selves and communicating in a world that is not entirely real.

Overuse of technology happens when technology controls the user rather than the user controlling the technology. For some, it's the constant attention that one needs to show their "life statuses," for others, it's the reward of points or achievement. Gamification, the application of typical elements of game playing (e.g., point scoring, competition with others, rules of play) to other areas of activity, typically as an online marketing technique to encourage engagement with a product or service, has now been identified as an addictive piece. So many applications do this to entice us to participate.

Humans need to feel included and that we belong. The fear of missing out (FOMO) effect is strong. When some of us disconnect, reality sets in and our mental health is affected. Whether it's anxiety, stress, depression or our self-esteem. The self-assessment at the beginning of this book can help identify problems, and there are many resources online if you or someone you know falls into a severely addictive category.

Being in a position to lead a team experiment allowed Patricio to see how difficult it was for some employees to take some time away from their devices at work. The team members who embraced freedom from their devices had the opportunity to engage in human-to-human conversation, which encouraged more communication offline both at work and at home. Could this be an experiment that other organizations take part in? Could more brainstorming and creative ideas be brought forward to solve real problems if this took place? How would employees at your place of work react to such a program? Many workplaces are not set up to allow employees time away from a PC or a phone. Break time gives us back that opportunity, but what do we often do? We pick up a device to pass the time rather than conversing with someone.

Patricio Martinez Aguirre
Performance Coach
Chile

Technology has become a work tool for me. It has facilitated connectivity, fast connections to obtain answers, consultation with peers or experts when I needed a quick response, and it keeps me in touch with family, friends and colleagues. Basically, we need information to be delivered fast, so we use text messaging.

I was the Latin American vice president responsible for a mental health program that had a "Less time in front of a screen" initiative. For this initiative we defined a series of activities over a ten-month period including website content, experts' presentations, increased exercise (especially walking), dieting guides, etc. It all culminated on a specific day called "Be Well Day." On the final day, we did a wrap-up of everything that was presented over the ten months along with a healthy breakfast where people were to leave their phones in a "Parking Lot." There were people that did not follow this, others refused it and some got really angry and upset about what they felt from the beginning was a nonsense idea!

People, in general, are attached to their mobile phones. It's like a part of their wardrobe. We can forget anything when we leave home except for our mobile! The fastest animal on the planet is a human going back to where they left their cell phone.

I had a great experience with the mental health program and the "Parking Lot" idea. Blocking computers and screens before 9:00 a.m. forced people to talk, coordinate between each other and even use a whiteboard for brainstorming, which gave the opportunity to develop ideas and process information collectively.

In the future, our phones could replace personal computers, and having this as a portable tool will force organizations to rethink the way their employees work. I do not only mean home office or

> telework. I mean the leadership must change how they instruct and delegate and how tech will mutate to different deliverables. Task issues would likely go to a cloud-based platform, and employees, wherever they are, will take the tasks and complete them whenever they want. This will mean less human-to-human connection.

Are we all addicted to technology? If you have gotten this far in the book, you'll probably know for sure. We're likely all addicted to some degree, so it is time to disconnect and find other ways to connect and communicate. Here are some basics we can start with.

Be Aware

First, and foremost, be aware and fully conscious of what is actually happening around you with regards to technology and what the effects are on you and your family. Look for the signs of addiction and measure time spent on technology. Reading this book is a start.

Record how much time you are spending on your device. The iPhone, for example, has a Screen Time widget in the settings that (when turned on) will tell you how much time you've been on your iPhone or iPad. Parents can place limits for kids, and when they spend too much time scrolling through TikTok, for example, it will shut off. We can also place those limits on our own use.

At the end of each week, you'll get an automatic report detailing how often you or your child used the device, as well as the percentage of time spent on apps with specific categories, such as social networking, games, entertainment and productivity. There are many free screen time apps available for download. If you are a parent, try Screen Time Labs[52] or Freedom[53] so you can gain control over your relationship with technology. Freedom has over two million users, and they posted some interesting research statistics on their website:

- Every time we check e-mail, a social feed or respond to a notification, our mind requires twenty-three minutes to refocus and get back on task.
- We're actually 40 percent less productive when multitasking. Multitasking may even decrease our IQ by ten points!
- Willpower is finite. We try to ignore or shut off the digital world, but it is intentionally designed to win the battle.
- Our brains crave the rewards—the tiny hits of dopamine—that keep us checking and responding.

Create "Sacred Time"!

Have a family meeting and discuss options about "sacred time" where there is no phone or technology use for a period during the day. Use that time to get together, talk or play. Increase buy-in by encouraging everyone to share their thoughts and ideas about when and how this would be done.

Model the manners and behaviour you want to see in those around you, especially your children. Make a deal with your children that you'll put your phone down at 5:00 p.m. if they do the same, and then agree to do something together.

Some examples of "sacred time":

- During meals. Have a everyone place their phone in a box on the table.

---

[52] Screen Time Labs; https://screentimelabs.com/
[53] Freedom; https://freedom.to

- In the car. Many cars now have the ability to connect phones to the car so calls can be on speaker so everyone can hear and chime in rather than each person on their own phones. However, texting is still a no-no whether it's on a screen in the car or on the phone. The focus should be on the driving. The Big Rule: no more texting and driving!
- On vacation. Expensive roaming charges can be a great excuse for not using the phones on a vacation. Just one could be used for emergency calls and navigation if you need it. Agree on a time at the end of a day when everyone can post their pictures on their favourite social media site.
- Before bed. Shut down screen time thirty to sixty minutes before bedtime. If you have young children, read them a story rather than using devices; children love that. Charging your children's phones in your room at night gives them a break from their phones. Buy yourself a good book, have some alone time with your partner or choose another way to wind down without a screen. Go to a favourite bookstore as a family and let everyone choose a book once a month for their bedtime routine.

There will need to be a little bit of give and take, but ensure you involve everyone in the decision-making process.

Find Alternative Activities!

My son is an exceptional video gamer. I'm told by adult friends that his ability to navigate through a game and conquer it is unbelievable. He constantly tells me how he can beat games in two hours. Asking him to reduce his game time is difficult as he identifies with this exceptional skill. He also loves board games and will jump at a chance to play Monopoly or Risk. He loves the challenge, is competitive and he typically wins (but not always!).

Exploring activities outside of technology is not as hard as you think. Explore some of the ideas below and replace those tech hours with something that gets you off a device or encourages human-to-human interaction:

- Play a board game
- Plan a party
- Create/buy an unexpected gift for a friend/family member
- Play an instrument
- Draw/paint
- Bake a treat
- Go to the theatre
- Gather some friends to play a sport
- Take someone out for lunch
- Workout
- Go for a walk or a hike
- Go for a bike ride
- Organize a clothing swap
- Go swimming
- Declutter and organize
- Take the dog for a walk
- Take a nap
- Start a journal
- Try something new like art classes or a sport you've always wanted to try

Check Out Your Community Centres and Local Activities in the Area

Community centres not only encourage families to participate in activities that are not related to technology, but they also encourage families to do things together. Community centres have a host of activities for a variety of tastes ranging from swimming to art classes that families can register in together. They also typically list support services, free events happening around town and clubs or associations to join. Take a look at your local community centre guide where there is sure to be something that entices everyone.

 Put Down Your Smartphone and Take Some Mental Pics Instead

We're so busy trying to get that perfect photo that we forget to just enjoy the moment! When on vacation, keep a journal, really look at the surroundings, take in the smells, savour the taste of the food (rather than taking a picture of the plate) be "in the moment" with yourself, your partner, your family. These are memories you will treasure much more than a snapshot!

Be a Tourist in Your Own Hometown

I lived in the Toronto area for a number of years before I realized I had never been to the CN Tower. When you are visiting a new city, you find it exciting to take in all the landmarks, eat the local specialties and speak with the local people.

Imagine visiting London, England. I was born in England and lived there until I was a young teenager so I saw most of the typical tourist sites like Buckingham Palace and Big Ben. However, I still have family that live there and haven't visited either of these popular tourist spots, so it should be on my list.

We take for granted what we have to offer a new visitor, and we become complacent and think, *I haven't seen it but I live here so I can visit it whenever I want to.* The thing is we never do.

Think of a place or event in your hometown or a city that is close by that you have never visited. Make a day of visiting it with the family, a partner or a friend. You will learn about the history and heritage, events that are happening and you might even meet someone new. And yes, use your phone to take a photo, but enjoy the experience and be in the moment rather than taking selfies all day long!

Learn the Art of Conversation

Most people think that communication is simply talking. Almost everyone has the ability to talk. From the time we are babies learning our first words, we desperately want to communicate with others. As parents we wait for the day when our children speak their first words and celebrate it when they do. I'm sure people who cannot speak would be ecstatic to get off their devices and have a human-to-human conversation.

We, unlike the rest of the species on this planet, have the ability to speak words. But speaking words doesn't mean we know how to communicate. Think of the best communicators you know or have heard. Think of the worst. As the next section explores, the art of conversation is about effective communication.

Juanita Jeavons
Stakeholder Relations Analyst, Economic
Development & Communications
Canada

My sons are twelve and fourteen and they both have a phone. The eldest one has a phone contract, and the younger just uses Wi-Fi at home or to call me or my husband. They both have their own Chromebooks for school.

My childhood was sheltered and simple in terms of needs, wants and desires. I feel that my kids are more knowledgeable about the world and the things that they want than I was at the same age. As a society, we are all being impacted negatively due to the amount of time we spend on our devices to be "connected" to people not near us and the world as a whole. We are missing out on those events and relationships that are closest to us because we want to "know everything." Mental health issues are on the rise, and the lack of opportunity for young people to develop face-to-face relationships will negatively impact their ability to create and maintain healthy peer and family relationships in the future.

When I am at work, I am fully immersed in technology. At home, I hope I set a good example, but I am sure that there is always room for improvement. I am that person who removes myself from technology for the most part. I try to instill a sense of connectivity within my family circle by being the one to encourage the conversations around the dinner table without allowing devices to be part of dinner.

Juanita, like a lot of parents, realizes that our childhoods were very different than the ones our children are living. And it's not just about walking to school, uphill both ways. As we have read in previous chapters, the statistics show real issues and challenges that result from always being connected to our devices. Real conversations are not happening. Juanita also knows that a mindful parent creates an environment in the home that encourages the family to step away from technology. She also recognizes she must set the example for her children.

Communication and the Art of Conversation

How did you communicate in your last connection with someone? Was it by telephone? E-mail? Text? Messaging via social media? Video conferencing? Snail mail? (Yes, this archaic form still exists, but when was the last time you received a handwritten letter or birthday card?)

All these forms of communication allow you to exchange thoughts, ideas and information, yet they cannot replace face-to-face interaction. If your last communication was face to face, I applaud you. As a facilitator of communication workshops, I find this topic to be one of the most important. Most people feel they don't communicate well, which is why this workshop is requested the most. In a time when a lot of communication isn't done face to face, we are losing the ability to communicate well. Why? It starts with the devices and programs we use every day.

Your Phone

The telephone allows you to focus on the words and the tone of your voice, however, there is no facial expression or body language that accompanies the words. In many corporate offices, customer service reps are asked to smile when they answer the phone so there can be a noticeable difference to the caller. It doesn't replace a genuine smile but has a similar effect.

Texting and E-mail

Texting and e-mail can be communicative when using emoticons and abbreviations. As I mentioned at the beginning of this book, it feels like we have gone back to using hieroglyphics, however, if you are not completely familiar with their meanings, there is an opportunity for a communication breakdown.

In e-mail, we CAPITALIZE to add tone of voice (although it comes across as shouting) and we use colour or italics to emphasize words. But no amount of smiley faces or LOLs can tell us what the person is really thinking and saying. We have all misinterpreted a text message or e-mail at some point in our lives. If we know this person, our thoughts may fill in the blanks because of a previous conversation or our mood at the time may not be the greatest, so we misunderstand the e-mail. We cannot visually see the other person, what they are wearing, the expression on their face, their posture, the tone in their voice or the look in their eye.

Face-to-face communication is the only way to truly connect, gain understanding and simply get the message across. Meeting face to face builds rapport in business relationships, connects on a personal level with a friend or family member and simply shows you are physically and mentally there—you showed up!

What is communication?

Communication is defined as: "A process of passing information and understanding from one person to another."[54] Effective communication takes place when the receiver of the message understands the message the way the sender intended.

---

[54] Keith Davis, Professor of Management at Arizona State University

This takes effort on both sides, so messages can be misinterpreted. This causes mixed messages, misunderstandings and, at times, missed opportunities on a personal and professional level.

So, whether it's verbal or written communication, getting your message across and conveying your thoughts and ideas effectively, as well as understanding the barriers that cause communication breakdown, is vital to survival in parenting, personal relationships and in the workplace.

Communication Barriers

When two people communicate, they've come together from different backgrounds, hold different values, employ different words and respond with different judgments and emotional reactions. People hear what they want to hear—or what they expect to hear—and this can lead to misunderstandings.

If effective communication "takes place when the receiver of the message understands the message the way the sender intended," the receiver of the message will most likely understand what the sender is saying by actively listening and responding with questions to clarify.

Being clear and using language that everyone understands helps, however, getting to know and understand the person you are communicating with can eliminate most communication barriers. Getting to know the person is what communication is all about. Understanding the basics of communication is the key, and it starts with the Three Channels.

Vinesh Rao
Student
Canada

I am the owner of a number of different electronics. This includes an iPhone, iPad and a MacBook. On a general day, I would say I spend around one to two hours on social media and the Internet. My friends, on the other hand, most likely spend up to six hours a day on the Internet.

I do feel a sense of information overload at times. I believe this is due to the constant and excessive amounts of data I take in when texting and playing around on the Internet. From the brightness of the screen to the overload of texts that I receive, my constant time on technology makes my brain feel overburdened.

So far, social media has been one of the biggest distractions in my life. As I sit down to study relax to go to sleep, I always feel an urge to look at my phone for new posts on Snapchat or Instagram. My constant time on social media has also added stress to my life due to the pressure I have to answer messages from my friends or check out the latest posts from celebrities. When I have friends over ensure we engage in activities that don't involve technology like physical games and conversations.

My sister is eleven, and she and her friends are addicted to apps like TikTok. She's on it all the time, sometimes till midnight. She could be doing so many other things.

Taking a look at my friends and family while they are on their devices, it is clear that they have no real care or perception of the real world at the time. All they care about are the messages they receive on their phones or electronics. This makes our relationships blander since their main focus is social media and not on conversing and interacting.

> Excessive use of social media is a big issue in our society. I'm on a mission to get kids to interact again, build their social skills and manage the stress that overuse of technology brings.

Vinesh's experience is similar to his peers. There are so many options—Instagram, TikTok, YouTube and so on—to keep teens distracted. These online connections don't end, and it's a vicious cycle that is hard to break. Does Vinesh speak for teens that are feeling overwhelmed, overloaded and trying to keep up with their friends and family who are always online? Would they like to disconnect and engage in other ways? If so, do they know how to communicate well?

The Three Basic Channels of Communication: Verbal, Vocal and Non-Verbal (Body Language)

The Verbal Channel: Words

Do you know many words there are in the *Oxford English Dictionary*? Here are three key numbers:

- More than one million total words
- About 170,000 words in current use
- 20,000 to 30,000 words used by each individual person

We use the same words all the time when there is probably a better word that we don't realize could describe what we really want to say. This is especially true when we know who we are speaking with because different words resonate with different people. Adjusting our words helps ensure better understanding.

Some quick tips to consider:

- Watch Your "But": Use the word "however" rather than "but," which sends a more negative connotation.

- Avoid Telling: Say "I think" or "I feel," not "You should." You've probably had a conversation where you someone said, "You should just tell him," or, "You should have taken the job." This insinuates that the receiver of the message didn't know what they were doing or they need to be told what to do. This puts them on the defence. Instead, say, "I feel you might have missed an opportunity."

- Don't Use Jargon and Acronyms: "FYI. It's a BYOB and don't forget to RSVP, OK?"

  I understand this sentence. However, if I was inviting someone who was a newcomer to this country, they may not understand a word I said. I hear salespeople selling everything from shoes to cars who use acronyms and jargon not realizing that while they think they are sounding knowledgeable they are losing their connection with their customers who don't know the language.

  Use the same language as your audience whether it's your child or a partner. Using technical terms or acronyms with someone who is not familiar with these terms won't get your point across.

- Conversation Cushions!: People like it when you use their name because it makes them feel important and shows them that you remembered. It personalizes the conversation. A tip on how to remember someone's name: say the name five times over the course of a conversation. For example, "So glad to see you again, Judy," and, "Judy, you were amazing at that event, so organized." And so on.

- Stay Positive: Parents will most likely agree that saying "No" is a regular thing and it doesn't always go over well or achieve the result they wanted. Plus, it's a negative. Staying positive in a conversation helps ensure communication doesn't break down.

  For example, instead of, "No, I can't give you a ride right now," try: "I can leave in an hour once I'm finished making dinner. How about that?" It's also easy to say, "I don't know." Remember when you had your first job and you really didn't know anything? This phrase was certainly relevant, however, a much more positive and knowledgeable response is, "Let me confirm/verify that and I'll get back to you."

  One response I hear constantly that bugs me is "No problem." It is a negative statement, so why not say, "Happy to oblige," "Of course, happy to," or "It's my pleasure."

- From the Other Point of View: We all want to feel important, that we are not a burden on someone's time, that we are a priority as much as they are in the conversation. I especially see this when in a service situation. For example, Instead of, "We need your health card Identification, it's policy. I need it before I can pass you through," the administrator could say, "For your protection and quicker service, we ask that you provide us with your health card prior to seeing the doctor. Plus, there's no need to stay; you can go right after." Or instead of saying, "You need to pick up some chicken if you want me to make dinner tonight," try, "I'm making dinner tonight. You can relax, so would you pick up the chicken on the way home?"

- Initiating Conversation When Meeting Someone New: When meeting someone new, avoid asking closed-ended questions that can only be answered with "Yes" or "No." Ask open-ended questions that begin with who, what, where, when, why and how. Make a statement followed by a question. You can most likely think of many things to talk about, whether it's music, weather, current news or movies and TV shows. Try paying a sincere compliment. Stay away from religion and politics because you can never know a person's preferences.

  And stay in the know. If you know what's happening in your neighbourhood, the country and the world, conversations are a lot more interesting. You can talk about who won the game last night, when the next big blockbuster is coming out, when the new park is being built, and so on. Again, avoid religion and politics, and if the conversation gets heated, politely change the topic.

  "What do you think of the new park on 50th street?"

  "How did you get down here with all that traffic?"

  "When do you think the new Spiderman is being released?

  "That's an amazing jacket, where did you get it?"

- Be a Good Listener: A great communicator doesn't need to always be speaking. Listening skills are the key to great conversations. You have two ears and one mouth for a reason. Find out as much as you can from the person you are with. Listening skills are essential and will be explained in depth later in this chapter.

- People Love to Talk When They Have a Passion: Most people have something they are passionate about. At the start of my communication workshops, I ask everyone to introduce themselves and tell us something they are passionate about that most people might not know. The responses are always amazing. I've had everything from Elvis impersonators to psychics. If the person seems quite passionate about their hobby, ask more questions about it like why they started doing, how much time they spend on it and what tools they use?

- Find a Common Interest: Everyone loves to know that someone else shares their love for something. It's symbiotic. When I facilitate exercises in workshops that ask the participants to share their common interests or experiences, I have difficulty getting them back to the program. They are so engrossed in their conversations and are typically laughing and saying that they could talk for another hour. This is a great ice breaker.

Sharing a common interest opens up communication quickly. If you hear or sense there is a common interest, dive in and share your experiences, ask questions and watch the conversation take off from there.

- Smile: This sounds like a no-brainer, yet many of us go through our day without a smile on our face. We are intent on going from A to B and just need to get things done. When someone smiles at us, we typically smile back. No matter who you have a conversation with, a smile will always start it off on a positive note. Be sure it's genuine and stay positive.

How to Encourage Communication with Your Kids

- Make a meal together and take them with you to buy the ingredients.

- Take an interest in their hobbies and activities—a sport, an art piece and, yes, even if a video game. Play with them or cheer them on, but establish limits for screen time.

- Have them help you solve a problem. Start with: "I need your help…," or have them show you how to do something.

- Share a mistake you made; it shows you are human and it happens.

Just as there are tools to help conversation flow, there are some no-nos that derail it. We have all experienced these at one time or another, so be conscious that you are not committing them.

Interrupting Someone and Finishing Their Sentences

This typically happens when someone is excited or impatient, and it can be annoying to the person speaking. If you actively listen (which involves paying attention to the conversation, not interrupting, and taking the time to understand what the speaker is saying) and even bite your tongue (figuratively, of course!), your conversations will be much more enjoyable.

Continuously Talking

Some people like to hear the sound of their own voice, and we've all been in a conversation where the talker likes to talk. They rarely ask a question, and if they do, they redirect the answer back to themselves. Don't be this person because it means you're making a speech not holding a conversation.

Gossip

Even though you may feel you are creating a bond with someone, gossip can go bad quickly. Break the cycle and don't indulge because someone at the other end eventually gets hurt.

John Lintott, BEd
Parent and Foster Parent, Income Assistance Worker
Canada

My daughter and I use social media sparingly. It feels like we use it less than our peers, and that sometimes creates tension. For me, the tension comes from being out of the loop or not knowing how to respond or use social media etiquette. For her, it's being left out when she feels like she is being left behind by her "more mature" peers.

As far as tech time habits, I manage mine poorly. I often find myself trying to de-stress by being on my phone, and that comes at the cost of ignoring my daughter. She, however, helps motivate me to get off my device. She's only eight, but she and I both know we are too easily consumed by screen time, and we try to motivate each other to use it less. She picked up this habit from her mother.

Regarding screen use, I could categorize our family friends into two groups: educators and non-educators. Our educator friends, mostly early childhood educators my wife befriended as part of her career, try to limit screen time and are able to do it successfully because they have training, education, and experience in how to avoid screen time. Many of our non-educator friends are not aware or are indifferent to the hazards of too much screen time. If they do know, they are not fully equipped to mitigate it. Even our family, who knows the hazards and possesses the knowledge to do better, encounters the same common and powerful enemy that all parents do: lack of time. If both parents work or the family has only a single working parent, screen time becomes a poor quality but lifesaving babysitter that placates the children while the parents get work done (even if that work is simply "decompressing" from a stressful day).

To put it simply, many of our friends know of the dangers and want to do better, but they lack the training, resources or time to do better.

If knowing about tech addiction is half the battle, then we're a quarter of the way there. Lately, I've seen the tide turning with regards to screen time, but that may simply be due to the early childhood education circles we run in. Still, things like Facebook have been exposed as dangerous, and public opinion seems to be viewing things like social media in general as a useful but hazardous tool of our time.

As for how to mitigate it—geeze, if you have an idea let me know. The problem is, screen time is fun and easy, and that's what makes it so dangerous. Having simple fun used to be kinda hard: you had to build something, run around, meet new people and make mistakes. Now you can have all that fun without leaving your home, without making it hard for yourself, without making mistakes. In essence, without experiencing growth.

The only way I can think of to mitigate the problem is to find something you enjoy that doesn't involve a screen, like doing sports, art or music. And while you're doing these things, just enjoy them for what they are and resist the urge to constantly share them on social media. Start treating your phone and devices like tools that spend more time in your pocket and less time in your hand.

Claudia Lintott, BA, ELCC
Parent and Foster Parent, Early Childhood Educator
Canada

As someone in an administrative position at work who is always connected, my child's life is less connected and I am glad for that. Whether it's social media, e-mail or text messages, I have felt the need to be always connected, and it's not a good feeling. One of the best decisions I ever made for myself and my family was to delete the Outlook app connected to my work e-mail from my phone. I hate the Pavlovian response I feel to my cell phone when it vibrates because it takes me away from what is most important, which is the people in front of me.

During the COVID-19 pandemic, my husband and I made the uncharacteristic decision to allow her to access Messenger Kids in order to stay connected with her best friend. While I know she wants to be more connected, especially having been given some access to it, I appreciate that she doesn't ask for it consistently.

Generally, parents want better for their children than they do for themselves, and this is definitely one realm where I am glad that her connectedness is lower. But as she gets older, it's going to be more of a challenge as she has expressed that her peers have much more access to media and technology than she does.

I do okay at managing my tech time, but I can absolutely do better. I am often the one who suggests activities other than screen time and tries to regulate both my husband's and my daughter's use. We have a "no tech at the table" rule for meals; the only exception is if we receive a work phone call or text message. I try to keep my phone put away when I'm with our kiddos, but I also slip into pulling it out. I've often wondered if I should buy a proper camera because that's usually why I pull out my phone when I'm with the children. But then I get distracted. During the COVID-19 pandemic, I started using screen time more as a "babysitter," especially when I had to work from home without any help in the house. I feel I set a decent example, but my use certainly increased.

As far as unplugging, I feel that some do better than others. It's tough: parents are overworked, exhausted and lacking the resources to be able to make choices other than turning on the TV. And when I say resources, I mean they are lacking the community needed to be able to avoid plopping kids in front of the TV. There are often no additional family members in the home who could help with childcare, you can't send your children outside to play by themselves without judgement and potential concerns about lack of supervision, and the more urban the setting, the less safe it is.

I feel that my friends whose background is in early childhood education at least understand why we shouldn't rely on screen time. They likely do better in curbing screen time, but they also face those challenges with their older children and express that it is more and more challenging when technology is required to participate in school and stay connected with friends.

We all need to get more comfortable with boredom. If we can't even stand in line at the grocery store or get through a lull in conversation without pulling out our phones, what chance do our kids stand? When children get bored, instead of allowing screen time, recognize that if you can get through the discomfort of their persistent demands, they will be okay! They will find something else to do.

Be open with your kids about why screen time can be detrimental, and have them help you generate parameters around usage. My husband came up with a cool system of helping our daughter decide how to spend her screen time. On the weekend, she can have up to three hours of screen time which is broken down into ten-minute bubbles. An episode is two bubbles, a movie is four or five. So we set the three-hour limit, but she decides how to spend that time. Weekends can be a bit more fluid, but we have are stricter during the school week.

Engaging in screen time with your children is important. It's one thing to sit them in front of the TV or computer, but it's a different experience to watch with them and to talk to them. Taking an active role with your child can help ensure that what they're engaging is developmentally appropriate. You can talk them through what they're seeing so that they're not just passively receiving what is on their screen.

One concern I have is that I can only set parameters around her screen time at home. If she's at a friend's house, or even at school, I have absolutely no input. I was so disappointed when I found out that her school puts on TV during lunch hour while the children eat *because there's no lunch monitor due to funding*. So, while I am trying to ensure less screen time at home, the school made a different decision.

It would be of benefit to all parents to learn at least a bit about child development or be aware of the effect of screen time on the brain. When children have tantrums or meltdowns when the TV is shut off, we need to understand that it's not just children "misbehaving." We have a strong response to screen time and when the dopamine starts flowing, turning it off can be really hard, especially for little ones who are still learning to regulate their behaviour.

John and Claudia are parents who get it! Does it help that they are part of a group of child educators? Sure. Lack of training can have an impact, however, gaining awareness has to come before finding solutions. It begins with looking at our own behaviour and making changes. Claudia deleted the Outlook app on her phone, which set the example. Taking charge with screen time can be tough, and there is some great advice and solutions here from an educated couple who also struggle with it. Ideas like communicating with your children while you both watch TV and engaging them in conversation rather than simply plopping them in from of the screen is taking that active role. Their commitment to these techniques and reducing access and screen time for their daughter—and sticking to it—shows they know what the consequences are if they don't.

Speaking with Your Kids about Technology

If you are like most parents, you have repeatedly heard that your kids desperately need a phone. That all their friends have them. That they need them for various legitimate reasons. When the day comes to purchase their first phone, this is the time to discuss the rules and limits. For example, when it comes to communication, one rule could be no phone at the dinner table. Or when someone is trying to speak to you, put the phone down and listen. Time limits could mean no texting after 9:00 p.m.

When you have the conversation with them, let them know that technology is not evil; we all use it, but it's *how* we use it that can make the biggest difference. Include them in the development of the rules and limits and make a deal with them about appropriate behaviour. Children are more likely to stand by them if they do.

Rules and limits apply to everyone, so set the example! Otherwise a deal is moot.

The verbal channel of communication brings the focus to *what* we say and the words we use to communicate with the ultimate goal of creating understanding. If the words we use are not understood by the person we are speaking with, this leads to misunderstanding. This applies to all communication, whether we are speaking face to face or virtually. The verbal channel is only one of the three basic channels of communication. Next up is the tone of voice.

The Vocal Channel: Tone of Voice

You've probably heard the phrase "It's not what she said, it's how she said it." Tone impacts how people respond to you—positively or negatively. Think about that news anchor. Reading the news requires pace and good tone of voice. Depending on the story they are reporting, the tone, pace and pitch of their voice changes.

 Why Won't Your Dog Listen to You?

Tone of voice is the only way you can speak with your dog. You don't speak dog language, so when you do speak to a dog, what they are hearing is "Blah blah blah blah blah blah." The best way to describe tone is through this quick exercise.

Say to your dog: "You are a bad dog and shouldn't have destroyed my shoe" using a "good dog" (typically high pitched, soft, sweet and endearing). Then try praising your dog in your "bad dog" tone (typically deeper and stern). Watch the dog's reaction. A dog will respond to your tone not your words. Remember they really have no idea what you are saying, but they do understand your tone.

The Tone Switch Off

How you say something is just as important as what you say. Dogs are not the only ones that respond to the tone in your voice. Think of a friend, partner, parents, children, boss or teacher. Can you remember a conversation where the tone of the speaker was memorable? Was it condescending? Phony? Irritated?

Imagine someone asked you, "How are you feeling today?" and you responded with, "I'm doing OK. I'm feeling better." Now imagine you responded with the following negative vocal tones:

- Bored: Indifferent, uninterested
- Fake: Phony, not genuine
- Rushed: Quick, hurried
- Annoyed: Irritated, annoyed
- Timid: Uncertain, cautious

Now imagine answering with a more positive reply:

- Enthusiastic: Interested
- Sincere: Genuine
- Paced: Toned-down
- Relaxed: Easy-going
- Confident: Positive

Which conversation would you rather be a part of? The answer is most likely the second one. How many conversations have you had where the opposite was true? How many of these conversations have you demonstrated the vocal negatives?

Changing the Tone

Do you remember the first time you recorded a voicemail message on your phone? Did you like how you sounded? Most realize that their voice sounds different to what they thought. You don't hear the same thing inside your head as others do from the outside.

The best way to determine how you really sound is to listen to your tone and responses. To do this, record yourself during a conversation. Do you respond with any of the vocal negatives? And how do you really sound? The sound and tone of your voice should encompass the following:

- Enunciation: Clear pronunciation. Be sure you are pronouncing each word correctly. Listen for the "ums," "ahs," "likes," or "you knows." When these are said over and over, the listener starts to recognize them and they can become distracting.

- Volume: Breathing is important because proper breath support is the foundation of a good voice. When you exhale, project your voice but don't shout.

- Pitch: Aim for the middle range (typically a woman's voice gets higher when she is excited)

- Pace: Listen to news announcers and understand the pace they use. Speaking too fast implies anxiety, but too slow means you're overly cautious.

- Rhythm: Pause during a conversation for effect and include variety in your rhythm. Try not to be monotone and drawn out.

- Energy: Energy does not mean speaking fast. Try to average between 120 to 160 words per minute. We read faster than we talk, so don't talk as fast as you read. You can project enthusiasm by changing tempo, which provides variety. Be excited about what you are talking about and bring some emotion to the conversation if it calls for it.

These tips take time to perfect, so try focusing on a couple and see how it goes. They are great to try out in your everyday conversations, and at the very least it will make you more aware of your tone of voice and that of others. These tips are also important when speaking in front of a group. Speaking and presentation skills are great to have in your lineup of talents.

Which One?

Family time: Let's play a board game – too tired
Now in bed scrolling the Internet – looking at cat videos!

Romantic dinner and a night in a hotel ($500) – "Can't afford it!"
A new iPad ($500) – "Gotta have it!"

30-minute walk – "Too busy"
30 minutes on Facebook – "Where did the time go?"

It's about priorities. What are yours?

Non-Verbal Communication (Body Language)

The words we use and the tone of our voice are important, however, communication experts say that 55 percent of communication is body language, 38 percent relies on the tone of voice, and only 7 percent accounts for the words we use. Body language can be a powerful tool once you understand it. It can help you express yourself more clearly and help you understand what others are really saying to you.

We are constantly sending and receiving non-verbal signals, often without even knowing it. How we move, sit, stand, what we do with our hands, our eyes, the gestures we make—this is our body language.

Have you ever been in a group conversation when someone rolls their eyes at a comment? Or maybe you've had a conversation with someone who is staring at you with their arms tightly folded. If a friend is checking their phone or looking at the clock when you're telling them something deep and personal, what signal are they sending? How does this affect their communication with you?

Understanding body language enables you to read others, understand how they might be feeling and then respond to those clues. This type of body language creates a connection, openness and trust.

When we are able to "read" these signals, we can use them to our advantage. We can adjust our own body language so we appear more positive, engaging and approachable. Being aware of negative body language in others can allow you to pick up on unspoken issues or bad feelings. Understanding the following signals can help you communicate more effectively.

The Body

The way you stand, sit, walk and hold your posture all contribute to the message you are sending. The way you tilt your head or when you place your hands on your hips are body movements that send a signal. When you roll your eyes at something that has been said, you may be saying, "That was a stupid remark." If you cross your arms over your chest, you could be showing resistance and suggesting that you don't agree with a comment. On the more positive side, if you are nodding your head, you are suggesting you understand.

Eye Contact

Eye contact says a lot about you and your intentions. When you look at someone, your eyes can say many things. You may be sending a signal that you are attracted to the person or you are indifferent. Maintaining eye contact is important if you are to keep the conversation going and so you can assess the other person's response.

Touch

One great example of touch is the handshake. Remember those? A firm handshake will tell your business associates that you mean business and affirm that you are equals in the conversation if you duplicate the firmness you feel. A limp handshake conveys weakness, shyness, non-confidence.

Show your teen how to shake someone's hand. This simple gesture is a wonderful way to teach a young person how to interact on a professional level as well as impress the receiver of the handshake; this can go along way for future interactions!

A warm embrace, a nudge in the arm, a fist bump or a pat on the head will send a message—positive or negative. What message do you want to send?

Facial Expressions

Whether you are happy or sad, in shock or angry, your face can express almost any emotion without you saying a word. Think of how actors have mastered the art of facial expression and how to express certain emotions so you can be aware of your expressions and what impact they have during a conversation.

Gestures

We use gestures daily without thinking. The "OK" symbol, a wave or a thumbs up are all gestures we use on a regular basis. When dealing with other cultures, however, gestures can mean different things, so be careful. See "Mixed Messages" for tips.

Space

A space invader is someone who gets inside your circle, which is typically about two to three feet around you. If you are in a relationship, then close quarters may not be an issue. Culture also plays a role here. For example, depending on the culture, a kiss can be a natural greeting or an invasion of privacy.

Mixed Messages and Cultural Differences

Most facial expressions like happiness, anger and surprise mean the same thing around the world. For example, a genuine smile can show happiness; wide eyes and an open mouth can show fear or surprise. But, as mentioned, your body language and other gestures can send unintended messages. Actions mean different things in different cultures. Being aware of these differences will help you avoid misinterpretation and embarrassment. If you plan on engaging with someone from another culture or visiting their country, check on the difference in gestures and body language. Below are just a few examples:

Thailand
The head is a sacred place. Touching the top of it is considered insulting.

France
The "OK" symbol with your thumb and forefinger means "worthless."

Saudi Arabia
Men hold hands as a sign of mutual respect and friendship.

China
Giving a clock as a gift might be the same as wishing bad luck for the recipient.

Several Asian Countries
Pointing as well as direct eye contact is considered rude.

In China, people make eye contact when they are angry, and it can mean you are challenging another person; it is a sign of disrespect.

Pointing is considered extremely rude in Malaysia.

In Vietnam, eye contact can be seen as a way of showing attraction to someone.

The Kiss
Kissing on the cheek once is fine in Scandinavia. In France, it's typically twice, one on each cheek. In Holland or Belgium, it's usually three.

Study the cultures and customs of the people you interact with before visiting or conducting business if you don't want to seem rude or embarrass anyone (including yourself!).

Communication Crashes

We have all had conversations where we knew the communication was breaking down and an argument ensued. Whether with a partner, a child, a parent or a co-worker, these communication crashes happen often and can spiral out of control. Being aware and recognizing the communication crashes can assist with moving past the argument cycle. See if you recognize any of the crashes below. I'm sure you will:

I'm superior (patronizing)	A mother who speaks to her grown child as if he were still a toddler.
I'm in command	Ordering rather than asking. Want co-operation? Ask rather than tell.
I'm telling you! (threatening)	If the advice or instruction is not carried out, something bad will happen. "If you don't call her you are going to regret it."
I'm a therapist	Stating that someone is this that type without really knowing their past or internal struggles. For example, stating that someone is "unfriendly" when, in fact, they are shy or not confident enough to speak up in a conversation.
I'm sarcastic	Being cynical or skeptical stops communication. When someone does something wrong and you say, "Well done!"
I'm an expert (unwanted advice)	Instead of offering people advice, let them ask for it. Try: "Can I offer a suggestion?"
I'm the judge	Assessing in a general way and not being specific. Be objective and stick to the facts. For example, rather than saying, "You are always late," you can say, "The last three times we agreed to meet at the mall, you haven't made it on time. Is there a better time to meet or a different place that's best for you?"
I'm vague	Get to the point rather than skirting around what you actually want to say. Be clear. People cannot read your mind.

I'm redirecting	You may feel uncomfortable, so you change the subject during a conversation. This may suggest that you don't care.
I'm right, right?	Pressuring people into agreeing or rushing through the conversation. This borders on bullying. An example might be, "You agree with me, right? Say you do."

The key to effective communication is mutual respect. Always ask yourself, "If I rephrase my response this way, will it gain respect or will it alter the person's self-worth?"

People remember what we say, and that impression can stick with them through a lifetime. We forget what we say sometimes five minutes after we've said it. Using the techniques described in the three channels of communication will help you avoid communication breakdowns. Just being aware of them now will help you identify them in the future for yourself, your partner, your children and anyone you wish to engage in conversation.

Emotional Intelligence

You may have heard of emotional intelligence more frequently over the last few years. Often referred to as EQ or Emotional Quotient, it is not like IQ or Intelligence Quotient. An IQ test measures reasoning and problem-solving abilities like mathematical skills, memory and so on. An EQ test is meant to reveal how well we have learned to manage the harmful and helpful effects of emotions.

There are proven benefits of being more emotionally intelligent. These include improved relationships, more confidence, improved mental health, sharper purpose and better performance overall. Daniel Goleman's book *Emotional Intelligence*[55] focuses on the fact that life is not about being intelligent. Success in life is determined by having a higher EQ than IQ. Having good communication skills is one part of acquiring a high EQ and, in turn, developing effective social skills.

The problem today is that our EQ is being drastically affected. The constant interaction we have with technology has taken over having an in-person conversation. Children, for example, are in a bubble when they are consistently on a device. Schools must implement rules about phone use, yet as soon as it's time for recess, the phones are out again. Few are interacting with others, so everyone's social skills are being impacted. This can lead to more isolation since there is less face-to-face interaction. Relationships and friendships become disconnected. When we are disconnected and prefer to spend time on a device rather than with family and friends, we lose the ability to read others, and we become

---

[55]   Emotional Intelligence, Daniel Goleman

less compassionate and less tolerant of other's feelings. We simply lose touch because we can't communicate effectively with people outside our tech bubble. This, in turn, can affect working with a team and collaborating with others, showing empathy, and a whole host of other challenges.

Children and teens are often not able to obtain the benefits of having EQ; it is typically something that is learned. If they are not able to practice due to constantly being in the bubble, how will it affect their future?

Listening

The word LISTEN contains the same letters as the word SILENT. Think about a situation where you later realized that you had *not* listened or understood what was being said to you. Maybe you were called to pick up something on the way home but you weren't really listening. Did you bring home the wrong thing? Did you go back to the person and ask them to explain again? How did they react?

These situations happen all the time and can cause minor or major communication breakdowns.

Maybe you were distracted by some minor point in a discussion and failed to understand or focus on the key point. Maybe you didn't confirm or check before you got off the phone. Maybe there was too much information to take in all at once, or maybe emotions got in the way.

So how can you avoid misunderstandings like this? This is where listening skills come into play.

Listening and Understanding

 The biggest communication problem is that we do not listen to understand, we listen to reply.

Developing our listening skills is the key to communicating effectively. Again, we have two ears and one mouth for a reason. Most of us don't do a great job of listening. Some of us like to hear the sound of our own voice and others are waiting for you to finish what you are saying so they can have their say. Great listeners practice the following skills:

1. Show interest

- Let the person know you are listening and paying attention.
- Stop what you are doing. That means put your phone down—face down!
- Make eye contact.
- Use the right body language: face the person, nod your head when appropriate, unfold your arms.
- Make comments to show you are listening. "WOW, I see that. What else happened?" or "Tell me more."

2. Focus on the key issue

- Be patient and wait to comment rather than jumping in on the first point. There may be more to tell that you haven't heard yet.
- Clarify what the main issue is by asking questions. For example, "Is the main problem that your car is not working?"

3. Summarize and check

- Use "active listening."
- Fully concentrate, understand, respond and then remember what is being said.
- Summarize or rephrase what the person has just said by saying it back to them.
- They will then know that you are listening, so if you got the message wrong the person can correct you.
- For example, "So just to confirm, you would like me to give you a ride to work tomorrow at 8:00 a.m.?"

4. Read between the lines

- Find a pattern of what the person is really saying by listening carefully.
- Can you identify some common issue or pattern running through the conversation?
- Watch the other person's body language; do they shift positions when the topic comes up or do they change the subject? This may indicate that there is an issue.
- Read the clues and make a comment like, "It seems that this is really hard for you."

5. Respond to feelings

- When someone is upset, angry, frustrated or annoyed, acknowledge these feelings and discover the reasons behind them. You are more likely get to the real issue if you respond to the feelings and then potentially help to solve the issue.

Communicating is more than just a text message. A true conversation with another person requires us to be present, physically and mentally in that space, listening and responding. We notice the tone in their voice, we watch their body language and we can sense excitement, and sadness and truly see the emotion on their face. Our devices take away this human experience.

Yen Mach
Mother and Business Owner
Canada

My kids are eleven and fourteen. They have iPads, iPhones and their own laptops—all necessities for them to complete their homework. They also have classes after school, so I like them to have their phone in case I'm running late or they need something. However, I made a rule that there are no phones when we eat. When we are with friends, they are not to be on their phones either. We want them to play and interact with each other. Not all of our friends feel the same, so they allow their kids to be on their phones. This makes it more difficult for us to enforce our rules.

In school, they have to use their PCs but not their phones (they have to be in their lockers).

My younger one doesn't really want a phone, but we make her carry it just in case she gets lost. I remember as a kid waiting for my parents for hours, and I'm sure it wasn't safe for me to be by myself. I've had to take my older one's phone away, especially when doing homework, but I don't think this is the solution because it doesn't teach them how to live responsibly with technology. I do believe that it is a necessity—not a luxury—because they will need technology to survive in the future. I think they miss out on some of the things we used to do, like board games, for example—things that are not tech related.

When we are at social gatherings, people are on their phones and not communicating in person, so I wonder why we are getting together in the first place. The phone is used as a false sense of security. They have someone to talk to and this gives them an excuse to not interact with anyone else. They don't need to communicate with the person next to them because they have their phone. This is sad.

I'm guilty of being on my phone more that I should be, and I certainly miss out on my own human interaction. For example, if I was on a bus or a plane before I had a phone, I would typically strike up a conversation with the person next to me. I don't now. I'm also guilty, like many of us, of picking up my phone as soon as I wake up in the morning, so within minutes of waking I am on a device. I've read books that say you should try to wait for thirty minutes after you wake up, so I did that for a while; then I went right back to my bad habits. I need to overcome it but haven't so far.

My daughter said that when she grows up, she's not going to be on her phone because we miss out on so many things. She also suggested that in the future people will judge you based on your technology social status and not your personality. They'll decide whether to be your friend or not based on how many likes you have. I've read that this is already happening in China. I've also read that there's a trend in Japan where people can't be bothered with a real relationship. You can rent a girlfriend, parents, a pet, but they are not real-life interactions, these are paid actors. Some men are even marrying robots. Real communication is stressful and you can't control the other person's emotions, so a robot is an agreeable replacement.

You only have to conduct an Internet search to see that many Japanese aren't getting married or having kids. Their population is declining. Maybe it's foreshadowing things to come for us all. A glimpse into the future maybe?

Like most parents, Yen understands her girls need to have a phone or an iPad for security reasons, for school and so on, and she made an effort to reduce screen time when at the dinner table or with friends. She admits that it is hard to commit to putting down her phone and has developed some bad habits that she is trying to overcome. Her daughter's insightful comment about not wanting to be on her phone when she grows up and that she sees a judgemental future begs us to look at the trends that are happening in the world that could shape our future if we don't make a change.

Hikikomori, Population Decline and Robots

Hikikomori is a Japanese term that means a total withdrawal from society and seeking extreme degrees of social isolation and confinement. A person can isolate themselves in their homes for months or years at a time. They may appear unhappy, lose their friends, become insecure and shy, and talk less. Japan's welfare minister Takumi Nemoto referred to it as a "new social issue." The connection to the Internet, social media and video games addiction is not.

Although the connection between modern communication technologies (such as the Internet, social media and video games) and the phenomenon is not firmly established, they are at least a factor that can increase withdrawal from society.[56]

Japan's current population is declining at a rapid rate.[57] Although there are many factors that contribute to the

[56]   https://en.wikipedia.org/wiki/Hikikomori. "Hikikomori. Population Decline and Robots," n.d.

[57]   https://en.wikipedia.org/wiki/Aging_of_Japan. "Aging of Japan," n.d

decline, it warrants a look at hikikomori and addiction to technology.

Interestingly, to compensate for the population decline, Japan is pioneering the widespread introduction of robotics into many areas of society.[58] With plans to replace humans in many sectors like manufacturing and food processing, it is also aiming to introduce service robots that work closely with human beings in settings like care homes and hospitals.

If you would like a human companion in Japan, you can use a family rental service like Family Romance.[59] For a few hundred dollars plus travel expenses, you can hire a replacement for a friend or family member, alive or deceased. They provide companionship or they can accompany you to a wedding.

Is Japan leading a worldwide trend? Are we isolating more than ever? Will our human population decrease while non-human replacements take over? Can we count on a fake Uncle Joe to be there for us when times are tough? When there is a lack of communication and human connection, something is bound to take its place. We communicate every minute, every hour, every day but typically through a device. A device we have difficulty turning off or putting down. If we lose the ability to listen, communicate and simply have a conversation with a person sitting right in front of us, where does that leave humanity? If all communication exchange in the future happens via a device, will we disconnect completely?

[58] https://www.researchgate.net/publication/344815453_Japan%27s_Population_Decline_and_the_Robotics_Revolution. "Japan's Population Decline and the Robotics Revolution," n.d.
[59] http://family-romance.com/friend.html. "Family Romance," n.d.

If you or anyone you know is constantly connected to a device, "disconnecting" will be a challenge. We all need a break—a digital detox—to reconnect with the people around us. And when we do communicate, we need to do it the right way. First, engage in a non-tech activity.

There are so many activities we could be engaged in that have nothing to do with technology. Many were listed at the beginning of this chapter. What are some things you could be doing alone or with family or friends that are not tech related?

We all communicate, but effective communicators use the strategies I've outlined well. Can you recognize the three channels of communication? What are you displaying, and what do you see in others? Do you actively listen or are you just waiting for the other person to stop talking so you can speak? When you listen, do you really understand? Are you willing to use the techniques to gain understanding?

Are your children's social skills lacking? What communication techniques can you use when speaking with your children? What can you teach them (once you get them off their devices) about how to interact with others and communicate well?

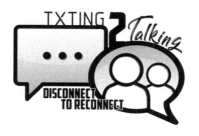

CHAPTER EIGHT

Your Challenge
and the Pledge

Challenges make you discover things about yourself that you never really knew.

Cicely Tyson

Personal Pledge: Phone-Free Sunday

After presenting at local schools, it was clear that students and teachers understood the message of *Txting 2 Talking* and "Disconnect to Reconnect." Most were open to using the tools and techniques to step away from their devices, but I needed a commitment from them.

My program evaluation comments were very positive, and many participants affirmed their need to step away from their devices, so I developed the No Cell Sunday Pledge and began distributing it after the sessions. My participants had no issues signing the pledge.

It's up to you to make the commitment. Read the pledge, sign the form and post it somewhere you can see it, like on the fridge or in the hallway.

You are in control.

You CAN decide to put your phone down and
Disconnect to Reconnect.

Life is what happens when you put your phone down.

Look at the REAL world around you, not through a screen.

Can you commit to unplug for an hour, an afternoon or a day?

No Cell Sunday
PLEDGE

I, _____,

(Your Name)

hereby pledge to commit to a **No Cell Sunday** on

_____

(Day/Date)

starting at _____ and ending at _____.

(Start Time)   (End Time)

✓ I will explore other activities to do with friends and family using examples from the *Txting 2 Talking* program.

✓ I will make an effort to find out more about the people around me by asking questions and **really** listening because I want to know who they really are!

✓ I will remember that my phone is a thing, a tool. It doesn't replace human-to-human, face-to-face interaction.

✓ When I pick up my phone again, I will realize that the person in front of me is more important and that no matter what the text message is… it can wait!

Spread the Word!
Share your experience on social media using #nocellsunday and encourage a friend to do the same.
Then get off your phone!
Pledge to take many more **No Cell Sundays**!

CHAPTER NINE

The Final Say

Look at a day when you are supremely satisfied at the end. It's not a day when you lounge around doing nothing; it's a day you've had everything to do and you've done it.

Margaret Thatcher

I am finishing this book just as we are coming out of our homes (depending on where you reside) from the throes of the COVID-19 pandemic. I joke with my friends and family that even the diehard introverts who were happy to stay home and isolate at the beginning of the pandemic are getting antsy and relishing the day when they can once again connect in person with their family, friends and co-workers.

The last few years have propelled us forward as far as technology in our workplaces and homes is concerned. We all knew we were heading in a more tech-focused direction eventually, but we didn't expect to get there so soon. Today, I can facilitate a workshop via Zoom or attend a meeting via Microsoft Teams. I can call my mother like I used to, but I can also see her, albeit through a screen. I could have done all this before the pandemic, except when push came to shove, I did it on a regular basis. I can have a phone consultation with my doctor so there's no need to take a morning off from work. I can work from home and have my groceries delivered. Sadly, I was also able to attend a virtual funeral for my cousin in England who died from complications due to COVID-19.

Arriving on the scene now is Artificial Intelligence. I did ask an AI-powered chatbot a couple of questions the other day and received some pretty interesting answers! AI is coming, what will that mean for us humans, will it leave us better off or not?

I think of the quote from the author Joel Barker from his book *Paradigms: The Business of Discovering the Future*: "The paradigm has shifted, and when the paradigm shifts, everything goes back to zero."

The paradigm has shifted and a new age is upon us. Technology has taken over so we can continue living. During the pandemic it allowed many of us the opportunity to slow down, get things done around the house and take stock of our lives. It also impacted others as far as mental and physical health and relationships and this is on going.

We need to reconnect in person, face to face, now more than ever. If you remember wearing a mask, then you remember how it hindered our ability to read emotions. This impacted how we communicated. When we finally removed the mask, it was a freeing experience to say the least. Giving a hug, a kiss, a reassuring arm around the shoulder, a high five (a real one, not an emoji), a hip bump, a dance with a partner, a handshake or a fist bump are things only humans can do; this basic need to reconnect is overpowering right now.

Questions we need to ask ourselves: Are we addicted to our devices because we are bored? Are we just multitasking? There is a lot going on in our lives and in the world, is our attachment to our devices a coping mechanism, a way to destress, detach and cope? Is this a teen problem or are we all struggling?

Disconnecting from our technology will never completely happen because we need it, we want it and it makes our lives easier, but we also crave human-to-human interaction. For all the parents out there: if you have lost the ability to connect and communicate with your children, try some of the suggestions in Chapter Five. Find that sacred time when you can all put your phones down and connect. I know that no matter what device they are on, they will likely agree to play a board game, go for a bike ride or bake a treat with you. So, take advantage of all the activities that require you to be with someone and experience that connection. Disconnect from your device, stop scrolling, messaging and texting. Actually shut down your phone and reconnect like you have never done before.

Humanity needs it.

Kathryn

My phone box in my family room. Yes it is
used, when I make a point of it.

My office - 2 laptops, 2 phones and an iPad. I get it!

At the restaurant, phones in the middle of the table

Spend quality time with your fur babies! I usually walk with my son, we talk and spend time with our dogs so this doesn't happen. We wanted to show you what we see sometimes.

Digital Doping, by JRL.

ABOUT THE AUTHOR

 Kathryn has gained more than thirty years of experience in sales and corporate executive management as well as developing and facilitating training programs in sixteen countries. Kathryn has received many accolades over the years, including national and international awards for sales achievement and, most notably, a training excellence award from the Canadian Society for Training & Development. She was formerly the president of the Durham Home & Small Business Association in Ontario, and she received a Business of the Year Award through that association.

Kathryn moved to Cold Lake, Alberta, and served as the small business advisor for the Rural Alberta Business Centre. During this time, she received two awards from the Economic Developers of Alberta; one in 2016 for the RABC Business Incubator, and the second for "Raising the Roof in Rural Alberta." Kathryn was also awarded the 2017 Women of Influence Award in the Business & Professional category.

Kathryn is the president and chief learning officer at Hotte Consulting Inc., as well as a business advisor and training consultant with Prospect Human Services. She is the past president of the Beaumont Chamber of Commerce, vice chair of Empowering

Women Entrepreneurs, and has also recently added actor to her resume by starring in the feature film *Moments in Spacetime.*

Kathryn is married to Richard, has three grown children, two step-children and a grand-daughter. She is also a pet parent to Coco.

APPENDIX 1

Additional Resources

CatchSec Technology Addiction Centre is on a mission to cultivate the right use of technology for the sake of stronger families, better productivity in the workplace, improved relationships between people, and enhanced connections between people. https://www.catchsec.org/

Venture Academy: Helping Teens with an addiction to technology. https://www.ventureacademy.ca/treatment-programs/electronic-addiction/

Help for video game and computer addiction. http://techaddiction.ca/

Internet and Technology Addicts Anonymous https://internetaddictsanonymous.org/

The NoSurf Reddit community https://www.reddit.com/r/nosurf/wiki/index

Online Gamers Anonymous http://www.olganon.org/home

Need Help Now helps teens stop the spread of sexual pictures or videos and provides support along the way. https://needhelpnow.ca/

The Center for Internet and Technology Addiction
https://virtual-addiction.com/

Ten Ways to Untwist your Thinking by David Burns M.D. *The Feeling Good Handbook*, his website, has helpful and free anxiety and depression resources.
www.feelinggood.com

Hotte Consulting Inc. offers dynamic in person and online workshops including pre and post knowledge evaluations and post program follow up. www.hottetraining.ca

Txting 2 Talking in person workshops for schools and colleges available including a fun and interactive communication game with prizes. Contact beinspired@hotteconsulting.com